Thomas P. Allen

**A Hand-Book of Classical Geography, Chronology, Mythology, and Antiquities**

Thomas P. Allen

**A Hand-Book of Classical Geography, Chronology, Mythology, and Antiquities**

ISBN/EAN: 9783337183059

Printed in Europe, USA, Canada, Australia, Japan

Cover: Foto ©ninafisch / pixelio.de

More available books at **www.hansebooks.com**

A

# HAND-BOOK

OF

## CLASSICAL GEOGRAPHY, CHRONOLOGY,

## MYTHOLOGY, AND ANTIQUITIES.

PREPARED FOR THE USE OF SCHOOLS,

BY

T. P. ALLEN AND W. F. ALLEN.

BOSTON:
SWAN, BREWER, AND TILESTON,
131 WASHINGTON STREET.
1861.

# PREFACE.

This work was undertaken in order to meet the want, which we had long felt, of a series of lessons in Ancient Geography, which should contain whatever was absolutely essential to the student, and no more. We have gradually enlarged our plan so as to comprise Chronology, Mythology, and Antiquities, always aiming to avoid the extremes of over-fulness and meagreness. Some portions, it will be seen at once, are designed only for reference. The geographical lessons contain also brief historical sketches, sufficient, we believe, to show the connection of each state with Universal History. They may be used with any good set of maps; — the references are to Long's, but there are a few names that will not be found in his Atlas.

In preparing this, we have of course made constant use of Smith's series of Dictionaries, and the Oxford Chronological Tables; but in all cases of doubt we have had recourse to the best and latest authorities within our reach. Our chief authority in Geography has been Kiepert; in Chronology, Grote and Mommsen; in Literature, Bernhardy; in Mythology, Preller; in Greek Antiquities, Grote and K. F. Hermann; in Roman Antiquities, Becker, Marquardt, and Mommsen. We would also express our great indebtedness to Professor Goodwin of Harvard College, who has kindly looked over the proof-sheets, and made many valuable suggestions.

# ABBREVIATIONS.

| | | | | | |
|---|---|---|---|---|---|
| M. | *Mountain.* | R. | *River.* | L. | *Lake.* |
| G. | *Gulf.* | Pr. | *Promontory.* | Id. | *Island.* |
| Str. | *Straits.* | S. | *Sea.* | C. | *Cape.* |
| K. | *King.* | Cf. | *compare.* | b. | *born.* |
| d. | *died.* | m. | *married.* | da. | *daughter.* |

\*\*\* Modern geographical names are in italics. The dagger (†) indicates a battle.

# CONTENTS.

## ANCIENT GEOGRAPHY.

|   |   | PAGE |
|---|---|---|
| I. | Northern Coast of Africa | 7 |
| II. | Egypt and Æthiopia | 8 |
| III. | Arabia, Babylonia, Assyria, Armenia, etc. | 8 |
| IV. | Media, Ariāna, Scythia, etc. | 9 |
| V. | Palestine, Phœnicia, Syria | 10 |
| VI.–VIII | Asia Minor | 11 |
| IX. | Islands in the Ægean Sea | 13 |
| X. | Thrace, Macedonia, Epīrus | 13 |
| XI.–XIV. | Greece | 14 |
| XV. | Islands West of Greece | 17 |
| XVI. | Sarmatia, Dacia, Illyrĭcum, etc. | 18 |
| XVII. | Germany, Britain | 18 |
| XVIII. | Gaul | 19 |
| XIX. | Spain | 20 |
| XX.–XXIII. | Italy | 20 |
| XXIV. | Rome | 23 |
| The Roman Provinces arranged Chronologically | | 24 |

## ANCIENT CHRONOLOGY.

|   |   | |
|---|---|---|
| I. | Oriental Period | 27 |
| II. | Grecian Period | 30 |
| III. | Roman Period | 34 |
| IV. | Roman Empire | 38 |
| Outlines of Ancient Chronology, by Centuries | | 42 |

CONTENTS.

## MYTHOLOGY.

### Grecian Mythology.

1. Theogony . . . . . . . . . . 45

#### I. *Olympian Gods.*

2. Zeus . . . . . . . . . . 45
3. Hera . . . . . . . . . . 46
4. Hephæstus . . . . . . . . . . 46
5. Athēna, or Pallas . . . . . . . . . . 46
6. Apollo, or Phœbus. — Phaëthon, Hyacinthus, Daphne . 46
7. Artĕmis. — Endymion. — Hecate . . . . . 46
8. Ares . . . . . . . . . . 47
9. Aphrodīte. — Adōnis, Eros, Psyche . . . . 47
10. Hermes . . . . . . . . . . 47
11. Hestia . . . . . . . . . . 47

#### *Lesser Deities of Heaven.*

12. Iris, Hebe, Nike . . . . . . . . . 47
13. The Hours, Astræa . . . . . . . . 47
14. The Graces . . . . . . . . . . 48
15. The Muses . . . . . . . . . 48
16. Asclepios. — Hygiēa, Ilithyia . . . . . 48
17. The Fates, Nemĕsis . . . . . . . . 48
18. Æōlus, Eos . . . . . . . . . . 48
19. Momus, Morpheus, Plutus, Hymen . . . . . 48

#### II. *Marine Gods.*

20. Poseidon. — Amphitrīte, Triton, Polyphēmus . . . 49
21. Proteus, Glaucus . . . . . . . . 49
22. Nereus, The Nereids . . . . . . . 49
23. Ino (Leucothea). — Melicertes (Palæmon) . . . 49
24. The Sirens. — Scylla and Charybdis . . . . 49

#### III. *Chthonian Gods.*

25. Cybĕle. — The Curētes and Corybantes . . . 50
26. Dionȳsus or Bacchus. — Ariadne, The Thiāsos (Pan, Priāpus, Satyrs, Sileni, Centaurs, Nymphs, etc.), Narcissus, Echo . 50
27. Demēter. — Proserpine, Triptolĕmus . . . . 51
28. The Cabīri . . . . . . . . . 51

### IV. *The Lower Regions.*

| | | |
|---|---|---|
| 29. | Pluto | 51 |
| 30. | The Rivers of Hades. — Cerbĕrus, Charon | 51 |
| 31. | The Judges of Hades. — Tantălus, Ixīon, etc. | 51 |
| 32. | The Furies | 52 |

### V. *Heroes and Demigods.*

| | | |
|---|---|---|
| 33. | Prometheus, Epimetheus, Pandŏra | 52 |
| 34. | Deucalion, Pyrrha, Hellen | 52 |
| 35. | Orpheus, Eurydĭce | 53 |
| 36. | Argos. — Io, Danăus, Perseus | 53 |
| 37. | Heracles | 53 |
| 38. | Thebes. — Cadmus, Eurŏpa, Œdĭpus, Antigŏne | 54 |
| 39. | Athens. — Cecrops, Philomēla, Theseus | 55 |
| 40. | Sparta. — The Dioscūri | 55 |
| 41. | Tantălus, Pelops, Atreus, Niŏbe | 55 |
| 42. | Marriage of Peleus and Thetis | 56 |
| 43. | Trojan War | 56 |
| 44. | Æneas, Ulysses, Agamemnon | 57 |
| 45. | Argonautic Expedition. — Jason, Medēa | 58 |
| 46. | The Amazons. — Hippolў̆te | 58 |
| 47. | Meleāger | 58 |
| 48. | Bellerŏphon. — The Chimæra | 59 |
| 49. | Admētus. — Alcestis | 59 |
| 50. | The Lapĭthæ | 59 |
| 51. | Amphīon and Zethus. — Dirce | 59 |
| 52. | Atalanta | 59 |
| 53. | Dædălus | 59 |
| 54. | Marsyas | 59 |

### ROMAN MYTHOLOGY.

| | | |
|---|---|---|
| 55. | Janus | 60 |
| 56. | Jupĭter. — *Spolia Opīma* | 60 |
| 57. | Mars. — Bellona. — *Ver Sacrum* | 60 |
| 58. | Quirīnus | 60 |
| 59. | Juno. — Lucīna | 60 |
| 60. | Minerva | 61 |
| 61. | Diāna | 61 |
| 62. | Neptune. — Consus | 61 |
| 63. | Vulcan or Mulciber | 61 |

## CONTENTS.

64. Liber Pater . . . . . . . . . 61
65. Ceres . . . . . . . . . . 61
66. Mercury, Termĭnus . . . . . . . 61
67. Venus . . . . . . . . . . 61
68. Vesta. — Vestal Virgins . . . . . . 61
69. The Penātes, Genius . . . . . . . 61
70. Saturn, Ops . . . . . . . . . 62
71. Vejŏvis, Diespīter . . . . . . . . 62
72. Mater Matūta, Bona Dea, Aurōra . . . . 62
73. Apollo Sorānus, Dius Fidius . . . . . 62
74. Pales, Picus, Faunus, Silvānus, etc. . . . . 62
75. Orcus, Dis Pater. — Manes, Lares, Lemŭres, Parcæ . 62
76. Dii Indigĕtes . . . . . . . . . 63
77. Pavor and Pallor, Libertas, Fors Fortūna, etc. . . 63
78. Juno Sospīta . . . . . . . . . 63
79. Apollo. — Sibyls . . . . . . . . 63
80. Cybĕle or Idæa Mater . . . . . . 63
81. Æsculapius . . . . . . . . . 63
82. Hercules, Castor and Pollux . . . . . 63
83. Bacchus . . . . . . . . . . 64
84. Isis, Serăpis, Mithras . . . . . . . 64

### Egyptian Mythology.

85. Ammon . . . . . . . . . . 65
86. Osiris. — Isis, Typhon, Apis . . . . . 65
87. Horus, Harpocrătes, Anūbis . . . . . 65
88. Phthah, Neith, Bubastis, Thoth, etc. . . . . 65

## ANTIQUITIES.

### Grecian Antiquities.

#### I. *Athens.*

89. Early Institutions. — Tribes, Phratriæ, Gentes . . 69
90. Institutions. — Trittyes and Naucraries . . . 69
91. Reform of Solon. — Timocracy, Classes . . . 69
92. Reform of Clisthĕnes. — Ten Tribes, Demes . . 70
93. Metics, Slaves, etc. . . . . . . . 70
94. Archons . . . . . . . . . . 70

## CONTENTS.

| | | |
|---|---|---|
| 95. | Ephĕtæ | 71 |
| 96. | Senate of Areopăgus | 71 |
| 97. | Dicasteries. — Heliæa | 72 |
| 98, 99. | Senate of Five Hundred. — Prytanes, Proëdri | 72 |
| 100. | Assembly. — Ostracism | 73 |
| 101. | Nomothĕtæ, Nomophylăces | 74 |
| 102. | Later Changes. — Four Hundred, Thirty | 74 |
| 103. | Liturgies. — Choregia, Trierarchy | 75 |
| 104. | Finances | 75 |

### II. *Sparta.*

| | | |
|---|---|---|
| 105. | Spartans, Periœci, Helots. — Syssitia | 76 |
| 106. | Kings | 76 |
| 107. | Ephors | 76 |
| 108. | Council | 76 |
| 109. | Assembly | 77 |
| 110. | Education | 77 |
| 111. | III. *Amphictyonic Council* | 77 |

### IV. *Games and Festivals.*

#### NATIONAL.

| | | |
|---|---|---|
| 112. | Olympic Games. — Pentathlon | 78 |
| 113. | Pythian Games | 78 |
| 114. | Nemean Games | 78 |
| 115. | Isthmian Games | 79 |

#### LOCAL.

| | | |
|---|---|---|
| 116. | Athenian Festivals | 79 |
| 117. | Other Parts of Greece | 79 |
| 118. | V. *Colonies* | 80 |

### VI. *Military.*

| | | |
|---|---|---|
| 119. | Athenian | 81 |
| 120. | Spartan | 81 |
| 121. | Macedonian Phalanx | 81 |

## ROMAN ANTIQUITIES.

### I. *Divisions of the People.*

| | | |
|---|---|---|
| 122. | Patricians, Plebeians, Quirītes, Popŭlus | 82 |
| 123. | Patrician Tribes, Curiæ | 82 |

| | | |
|---|---|---|
| 124. | Thirty-five Tribes | 82 |
| 125. | Reform of Servius Tullius. — Classes, Centuries | 82 |
| 126. | New Aristocracy, Equestrian Order | 83 |
| 127. | Gentes. — Names | 83 |
| 128. | Patron, Clients, Libertini, etc. | 83 |
| 129. | II. *Magistrates* | 84 |

### 1. Greater Magistrates.

| | | |
|---|---|---|
| 130. | Consuls. — Interrex, Proconsul, Lictors | 85 |
| 131. | Prætors | 85 |
| 132. | Censors | 85 |
| 133. | Dictator. — Magister Equitum | 86 |

### 2. Lesser Magistrates.

| | | |
|---|---|---|
| 134. | Ædiles | 86 |
| 135. | Quæstors | 86 |
| 136. | Tribunes of the People. — Viators | 86 |
| 137. | Triumviri Capitales, Apparitores | 87 |

### 3. The Empire.

| | | |
|---|---|---|
| 138. | Præfectus Urbi, Præfectus Prætorii | 87 |

### III. *Assemblies.*

| | | |
|---|---|---|
| 139. | Senate | 87 |
| 140. | Comitia Curiata, Comitia Calata | 88 |
| 141. | Comitia Centuriata | 88 |
| 142. | Comitia Tribūta | 89 |

### IV. *Priesthoods.*

### 1. The Great Colleges.

| | | |
|---|---|---|
| 143. | Pontifices | 89 |
| 144. | Epulones | 89 |
| 145. | Decemviri sacris faciundis | 90 |
| 146. | Augurs. — Haruspices | 90 |

### 2. The Patrician Colleges.

| | | |
|---|---|---|
| 147. | Rex Sacrificulus | 90 |
| 148. | Flamens | 90 |
| 149. | Salii. — *Ancilia* | 90 |
| 150. | Fetiales. — Pater Patrātus | 91 |

## V. Colonies, etc.

151. Roman Colonies . . . . . . . . 91
152. Latin Colonies . . . . . . . . 91
153. Municipia, Præfectūra, etc. . . . . . . 91
154. Provinces. — Senatorial and Imperial . . . 91

## VI. Military Affairs.

### 1. Before Marius.

155. The Legion. — Hastati, Principes, Triarii, Velites . 92
156. Maniples, Centuries, Turmæ . . . . . 92
157. Armor . . . . . . . . . . 93

### 2. Reform of Marius.

158. The Cohort . . . . . . . . . 93
159. Prætorian Cohort . . . . . . . . 93
160. The Camp . . . . . . . . . 93
160½. Triumph, Ovation . . . . . . . 94

## VII. Law.

161. Civitas. — *Caput* . . . . . . . . 94
162. Provocatio, Appellatio . . . . . . 95
163. Laws of the Twelve Tables . . . . . 95
164. Matrimonium — Confarreatio, Usus, Coëmptio. — Manus 95
165. Patria Potestas . . . . . . . . 95
166. Mancipatio . . . . . . . . . 96
167. Nexum, Addictus, Mutuum . . . . . . 96
168. Agrarian Laws . . . . . . . . 96
169. Sumptuary Laws . . . . . . . 97
170. Parricidium, Proditio, Perduellio . . . . 97
171. Courts. — Quæstiones Perpetuæ, Centumviri, etc. . . 97
172. Revenue. — Tribūtum . . . . . . . 97

## VIII. Festivals.

173. Feriæ Statīvæ . . . . . . . . 98
174. Feriæ Conceptīvæ . . . . . . . 99

## MISCELLANEOUS.

175, 176. The Ship . . . . . . . . 100
177. The House . . . . . . . . . 100

## CONTENTS.

| | | |
|---|---|---|
| 178, 179. | The Temple | 101 |
| 180. | The Theatre | 102 |
| 181. | The Amphitheatre | 103 |
| 182. | The Plough | 103 |
| 183–185. | Dress | 103 |

### TABLES.

| | | |
|---|---|---|
| 186, 187. | Measures of Length | 105 |
| 188, 189. | Measures of Surface | 106 |
| 190, 191. | Measures of Capacity | 107 |
| 192–194. | Weights | 107 |
| 195. | Money | 108 |
| 196, 197. | Grecian Money | 109 |
| 198–200. | Roman Money | 109 |
| 201–204. | Grecian Time | 111 |
| 205–209. | Roman Time | 112 |
| 210. | Dies Fasti, Comitiales, etc. | 114 |
| 211. | The Winds | 115 |
| 212. | Roman Prænomens | 115 |

### GENEALOGIES.

| | | |
|---|---|---|
| 213. | Family of Acrisius | 116 |
| 214. | Family of Tantălus | 116 |
| 215. | Family of Æăcus | 116 |
| 216. | Family of Deucalion | 117 |
| 217. | Family of Dardănus | 117 |
| 218. | Kings of Persia | 117 |
| 219. | Alcmæonĭdæ | 118 |
| 220. | Family of Miltiădes | 118 |
| 221. | Spartan Kings | 118 |
| 222. | Families of Antigonus and Antiŏchus | 119 |
| 223. | The Maccabees and Herods | 120 |
| 224. | Families of L. Æmilius Paulus and Scipio | 121 |
| 225. | The Metelli | 122 |
| 226. | The Carbos | 122 |
| 227. | The Scævŏlas | 123 |
| 228. | Family of Augustus | 123 |

# ANCIENT. GEOGRAPHY.

# ANCIENT GEOGRAPHY.

## I.

Northern Coast of Africa. (Map 23.)

**Mauretania.** Ruled by Bocchus in alliance with Rome, and afterwards by Juba II. Made into two Roman provinces, Tingitāna, *Morocco*, and Cæsariensis, *Algiers*, by Claudius. Conquered by the Vandals under Génseric, A. D. 429. — M. Atlas. — R. Mulŭcha. — Fretum Gaditānum, *Strait of Gibraltar*. — Columns of Hercŭles. — Massæsylii.

**Numidia**, part of *Algiers*. Famous for its cavalry. Under K. Masinissa, 2d cent. B. C., in close alliance with Rome. His grandson, Jugurtha, vanquished by Marius, B. C. 106. Made a Roman province by Caligŭla. — Cirta. — Massylii.

**Africa,** *Tunis*. Originally subject to Carthage, a colony of Tyre. Made a Roman province by Scipio Æmiliānus, B. C. 146. — Carthage. Utĭca. Zama.† Thapsus.†

**Regio Syrtica** or **Tripolitana,** *Tripoli*. — Leptis Magna. — Greater and Lesser Syrtis.

**Gætulia.**   **Libya.**

**Cyrenaica,** *Barca*. — A Greek colony, ruled for two centuries by the dynasty of the Battiădæ, then a republic (about B. C. 450). Afterwards a dependency of Egypt. United with Crete to form a Roman province. — Cyrēne.

## II.

### Egypt. (Maps 25 and 3.)

The narrow valley of the R. Nile, which at its mouth divides and forms the Delta. The monarchy was founded at a very remote era. Conquered by Cambȳses of Persia, B. C. 525. After the death of Alexander, Egypt was ruled by the Greek dynasty of the Ptolemies. Made a Roman province by Augustus, B. C. 30.

**Upper, or Thebais.** — Thebes, or Diospŏlis Magna. Syēne. Abȳdus, or This. Berenīce. — Id. Elephantīne. Philæ.

**Middle, or Heptanomis.** Memphis. Heracleopŏlis. Arsinŏe or Crocodilopŏlis. Hermopŏlis. — L. Mœris. — Pyramids.

**Lower.** — Alexandrīa. Naucrătis. Saïs. Pelusium.† Heliopŏlis. — Arabian G., *Red Sea.*

---

Æthiopia, *Nubia.* Probably a colony of Egypt. — Merŏe.

## III.

### (Maps 3 and 22.)

**Arabia.** (Petræa. Deserta. Felix.) Made a Roman province by Trajan. — Petra. — Persian G.

**Babylonia.** Empire founded by Nabopolassar, B. C. 625; overthrown by Cyrus, B. C. 538. — Babȳlon. Seleucīa. Cunaxa.† — R. Tigris. Euphrātes.

**Assyria.** Empire established in the 13th cent. B. C.; overthrown by Cyaxăres of Media, and Nabopolassar, B. C. 625. — Ninĕveh. Arbēla. Gaugamēla.†

**Mesopotamia.** Osrhoēne. — Edessa. Carrhæ.†

**Armenia.** Ruled by the native dynasty of the Arsacĭdæ from the 2d cent. B. C. until A. D. 428. — Tigranocerta. M. Ar′arat. Taurus. — R. Araxes. — Sophēne.

**Colchis.** — M. Caucăsus. R. Phasis.

**Iberia.**     **Albania.**    R. Cyrus.

## IV.

(Maps 22, 3, and 2.)

**Media.** Revolted from Assyria, 7th cent. B. C. — M. Zagros. Orontes. — Caspian Sea. — Atropatēne, *Azerbijan.* — Susiāna. Susa. — R. Choaspes. — Ecbatāna.

**Persis.** Revolted under Cyrus, and conquered Media (B. C. 559). — Persepŏlis. Pasargădæ.

**Ariana,** *Afghanistan* and *Beloochistan.* Parthia. The Empire of the Arsacĭdæ, founded in the 3d cent. B. C. Overthrown by Artaxerxes, or Ardishír, who founded the new Persian monarchy of the Sassanĭdæ, A. D. 226. — M. Paropamīsus, *Hindoo Koosh.* Carmania. Gedrosia.

**Bactriana.** **Sogdiana.** **Margiana.** **Hyrcania.**

**Scythia,** *Independent Tartary.* — M. Imāus, *Beloortagh.* — R. Oxus. Jaxartes. — Oxian Sea, *S. of Aral.*

India. — M. Emōdi, *Himalaya*. — R. Indus. Hydaspes, *Jeloom*. Hyphăsis, *Sutledge*. Ganges.

## V.

(Maps 21 and 20.)

**Palestine.** The kingdom of Solomon was divided, 10th cent. B. C., into those of Judah and Israel. The kingdom of Israel conquered by Assyria, B. C. 721; Judah by Babylon, B. C. 568. Afterwards subject to Syria; conquered by Pompey, B. C. 63, and finally by Titus, A. D. 70.

Galilee. — Nazareth. — L. Tiberias.

Samaria. — Sychem. — R. Jordan. — M. Carmel.

Judæa. — Jerusalem. Bethlehem. — L. Asphaltītes, *Dead Sea*.

Peræa.

**Phœnicia.** Of early commercial importance. Dependent on Persia, afterwards subject to Syria. — Tyre. Sidon. Ptolemāis, *Acre*.

**Syria.** Conquered by Assyria. After Alexander, an independent Greek kingdom under the Seleucīdæ; made a Roman province by Pompey, B. C. 64. — Antioch. Seleucīa. Palmȳra or Tadmor. Heliopŏlis, *Baalbec*. Damascus. Thapsăcus. — R. Orontes. — M. Libănus. Antilibănus. — Cœlesyria. Commagēne. Made a Roman province by Vespasian.

## VI.

### Asia Minor I. (Map 20.)

Mostly subject to Lydia, then to Persia, 6th cent. B. C.; after the overthrow of the Persian empire, divided into numerous states.

**Pontus.** A powerful kingdom. Mithridates VI. carried on war with Rome, B. C. 88–63, until subdued by Pompey. Partly united with the Roman province Bithynia; the rest made a province, Pontus Polemoniăcus, by Nero. — Zela.† — R. Thermōdon. Halys. — Pontus Euxīnus, *Black Sea.*

**Paphlagonia.** Subject to Pontus.

**Bithynia.** Ruled by native kings; made a Roman province, B. C. 74. — Nicomedia. Nicæa, *Nice.* — R. Sangarius. Thracian Bospŏrus, *Strait of Constantinople.*

**Galatia.** Colonized by Gauls, about B. C. 200; made a Roman province by Augustus.

**Cappadocia.** Ruled by kings generally in alliance with Rome; made a Roman province, with Lycaonia, by Tiberius. — Armenia Minor.

**Lycaonia.** Iconium, *Konieh.* Lystra. — Isauria.

## VII.

### Asia Minor II. (Maps 20 and 19.)

**Cilicia.** Infested by pirates; made a Roman province by Pompey, B. C. 64. — Soli or Pompeiopŏlis. Tarsus. Issus.† — R. Cydnus. Pyrămus.

**Cyprus.** An island, subject to Egypt under the Ptolemies; made a Roman province by Augustus. — Paphos. — M. Olympus.

**Pamphylia.** Made a Roman province, with Lycia, by Augustus. — R. Eurymĕdon.† Pisidia.

**Lycia.** — M. Climax. — R. Xanthus.

**Caria.** Belonged to Roman province of Asia. — R. Mæander.

**Lydia.** A powerful kingdom, comprising most of Asia Minor; conquered by Cyrus, B. C. 546. After Alexander, subject first to Syria, then to Pergămum. Afterwards part of the Roman province of Asia. — Sardes. — M. Tmolus. — R. Caÿster. Hermus. Pactōlus. — Pr. Mycăle.†

**Phrygia.** — Ipsus.†

## VIII.

### Asia Minor III. (Map 19.)

**Mysia.** Belonged to the kingdom of Pergamum, afterwards to Rome (province of Asia). — Ilium. — M. Ida. — R. Granīcus.† Scamander. — Propontis, *S. of Marmora.* Hellespont, *Dardanelles.* Ægē'an Sea, *Archipelago.*

**Pergamum.** A kingdom founded by Eumĕnes in the 3d cent. B. C., closely allied with Rome, and embracing most of the western part of Asia Minor. Attălus III. bequeathed his dominions to Rome, B. C. 133, which were formed into the province of Asia, B. C. 129.

**Greek Colonies.** Doris. — Halicarnassus. Cnidus.† — Ionia. — Magnesia on Mæander. Milētus. Ephĕsus.

Smyrna. Phocæa. Magnesia near Sipȳlus.†—Æŏlis. — Adramyttium. — On the Northern Coast. — Abȳdus. Lampsăcus. Cyzĭcus. Calchēdon. Heraclēa. Sinōpe. Cerăsus. Trapezus, *Trebizond.*

## IX.

### Islands in the Ægean. (Map 19.)

Thracian, Icarian, Myrtóan, Cretan, Carpathian S.
Thasos. Samothrace. Imbros. Lemnos. Tenĕdos. Scyros.
Belonging to Æŏlis. — Lesbos, Mytilēne.
Belonging to Ionia. — Chios. Samos. Lade.†
Belonging to Doris. — Cos. Rhodes. Carpăthus.
**Cyclades,** — Delos, M. Cynthus. Andros. Paros. Naxos. Melos.
**Sporades,** — Thera. Patmos.
**Crete.** Famous for its archers. Made a Roman province with Cyrēne, B. C. 67. — Cnossus. — M. Ida. Dicte.
**Eubœa,** *Negropont.* — Chalcis. Eretria. — Pr. Artemisium.† — Eurīpus.
Ægīna. Salamis.† Cythēra.

## X.

### (Maps 14 and 15.)

**Thrace,** *Rumilia.* Made into a kingdom by Lysimăchus, after Alexander's death; afterwards annexed to Macedonia. Made a Roman province by Claudius. — Lysimachīa. Abdēra. Byzantium. Sestus. Ægospotămi.†

— M. Hæmus. Rhodŏpe. — R. Hebrus. — Thracian Chersonēsus.

**Macedonia.** At the height of its power under Alexander, B. C. 330. Conquered (under K. Perseus) by L. Æmilius Paulus; — made a Roman province, B. C. 146. — Pella. Pydna.† Thessalonīca, *Salloníki*. Olynthus. Amphipŏlis. Philippi.† — M. Athos. Olympus. Cambunii. Pindus. — R. Strymon. — Thermáic, Strymon'ic G. — Chalcidĭce. Pæonia. Pieria.

**Epirus,** *Albania.* Flourished under K. Pyrrhus, about B. C. 300. Made a part of the Roman province Achaia; in 2d cent. A. D. became an independent province. — Ambracia. Dodōna. — M. Ceraunii. — R. Achĕron. Cocȳtus. Arachthus. — Pr. Acroceraunium. — Chaonia. Molossia. Thesprotia. Athamania. Dolopia.

## XI.

Greece I. Hellas. (Maps 15 and 16.)

Made a Roman province, Achaia, B. C. 146, by L. Mummius.

**Thessaly.** The tyrants of Pheræ held great power early in the 4th cent. B. C. Made part of the Roman province of Macedonia. — Larissa. Pharsālus.† Cynoscephălæ.† Demetrias. Pheræ. — M. Othrys. Œta. Ossa. Pelion. — R. Penēus. Sperchīus. — Pagasæan, Malian, G. — Vale of Tempe. — Magnesia. Perrhœbia.

**Acarnania.** — R. Achelōus. — Pr. Actium.†

**Ætolia.** Of little political importance until the formation of the Ætolian League, 3d cent. B. C. — Calȳdon. — R. Evēnus. — Pr. Antirrhium.
**Doris.**
**Locris.** Opuntii. Epicnemidii. Ozŏlæ. — Naupactus. Thermopȳlæ.†
**Phocis.** — Delphi. M. Parnassus.
**Bœotia.** A confederacy under the presidency of Thebes, whose power was at its height about B. C. 370. — Thebes. Orchomĕnus. Platæa.† Leuctra.† Coronēa.† Chæronēa.† Aulis. — M. Helĭcon. Cithæron. — R. Cephissus. — L. Copāis.

## XII.

Greece II. Attica. (Maps 16 and 17.)

The territory of Athens, which was the leading state of Greece, about B. C. 450. — Eleusis. Marăthon.† Phyle. Piræus. Munychia. Phalērum. Decelēa. Brauron. — M. Parnes. Pentelĭcon or Brilessus. Hymettus. Laurium. Ægaleos. — R. Cephissus. Ilissus. — Pr. Sunium. — Saronic G. — Pedion. Paralia. Mesogæa. Diacria. Thriasian Plain.

**Athens.** — Acropŏlis. (Propylæa. Parthĕnon. Erechthēum. Athēna Promăchos.) — Areopăgus. (Mars Hill.) Pnyx. Musēum. — Theatre of Dionȳsus. Agŏra. Thesēum (Temple of Theseus). Olympĭcum (Temple of Jupiter Olympius). — Ceramīcus. Academy. Lycēum. Stadium. M. Lycabettus.

## XIII.

Greece III.  Isthmus and Peloponnesus.  (Map 18.)

**Megaris.** — Megăra.  Nisæa. — M. Geranēa.
**Corinthia.** — Corinth. — Acrocorinthus.
**Sicyonia.** — Sicyon.
**Phliasia.** — Phlius.
**Argolis.** Consisting of cities over which Argos had a nominal supremacy. — Argos. Mycēnæ. Tiryns. Nemĕa. Epidaurus. Trœzen. — R. Inăchus. — Id. Calauria. — Pr. Scyllæum. — Argolic G.
**Achaia.** Of little political importance until the formation of the Achæan League, comprising all the Peloponnēsus except Elis, 3d cent. B. C. — Ægium. Patræ. — Pr. Rhium. — Corinthian G.
**Elis.** Important from its presidency over the Olympic Games. Generally allied with Sparta; afterwards belonged to the Ætolian League. — Elis. Pisa. Olympia. Pylos. — R. Penēus. — Triphylia.

## XIV.

Greece IV.  Peloponnesus.

**Arcadia.** Disunited states, without a head until the building of Megalopŏlis by Epaminondas, about B. C. 370. — Mantinēa.† Tegea. Orchomĕnos. Megalopŏlis. Phigalia. — M. Erymanthus. Cyllēne. Lycæus. Mænălus. — R. Alphēus. — L. Stymphālis.
**Messenia.** Conquered by Sparta, 8th cent. B. C.; restored

to independence by Epaminondas. — Messēne. Pylos. Ithōme. Stenyclārus. — R. Pamīsus. — Pr. Acrĭtas, *C. Gallo.* — Id. Sphacteria.† — Messenian G.

**Laconia.** The territory of the kingdom of Sparta, which had the hegem'ony about B. C. 400. Ruled by the tyrant Nabis, about B. C. 200; afterwards joined the Achæan League. — Sparta. Amyclæ. Sellasia.† — M. Taÿgĕtus. Parnon. — R. Eurōtas. — Pr. Malĕa, *C. St. Angelo.* Tænărum, *C. Matapan.* — Laconic G.

## XV.

Islands West of Greece. (Maps 15, 12, 9, and 4.)

In the Ionian Sea. — Zacynthos, *Zante.* Cephallenia. Ithăca. Leucas, *Santa Maura.* Corcȳra, *Corfu.* — Strophădes Ids.

**Sicily.** Colonized by the Greeks, and long contended for between Syracuse and Carthage. Made the first Roman province after the first Punic War, B. C. 241. — Syracuse.† Messāna. Himĕra.† Agrigentum. Panormus. Selīnus. — M. Ætna. Eryx. — Pr. Pelōrum. Pachȳnum. Lilybæum.

**Sardinia.** — Made a Roman province, together with Corsica, B. C. 238.

Corsĭca. Ilva, *Elba.* Melĭta, *Malta.* Liparian Ids. Ægātes Ids.† Pityūsæ Ids.

Baleăres Ids. — Famous for slingers. Conquered by Rome, B. C. 123.

2

## XVI.

(Maps 2, 3, 14, and 25.)

**Sarmatia,** *Russia, &c.* — R. Tanaïs, *Don.* Rha, *Volga.* Borysthĕnes, *Dnieper.* — Palus Mœōtis, *Sea of Azof.* — Tauric Chersonēsus, *Crimea.* — Cimmerian Bospŏrus, *Str. of Enikále.*

**Kingdom of Bospŏrus.** — A Greek kingdom which flourished several centuries; the chief granary of Greece. — Panticapæum.

**Dacia,** *Wallachia.* Made a Roman province by Trajan. — R. Tibiscus, *Theiss.* Tyras, *Dniester.* Danubius or Ister.

**Mœsia,** *Bulgaria.*

**Pannonia,** part of *Hungary, Sclavonia,* &c. — Vindobōna, *Vienna.* — R. Dravus. Savus.

**Noricum,** *Austria, Styria, Carinthia,* &c. — Noric Alps.

**Rhætia,** *Tyrol.* — Rhætian Alps. — L. Venĕtus, or Brigantīnus, *Constance.* — Vindelicia, *Bavaria.* Augusta Vindelicōrum, *Augsburg.*

\*\*\* The last four were made Roman provinces by Augustus.

**Illyricum.** A chief seat of pirates. Made a Roman province, 2d cent. B. C. — Scodra. Epidamnus or Dyrrhachium. — Liburnia. Dalmatia. — Mare Adrĭaticum or Supĕrum.

## XVII.

(Maps 25 and 5.)

**Germania.** Inhabited by wild and independent tribes, whom the Romans never wholly subdued. Two provinces, Upper and Lower, erected on the Rhine by Augustus. — Hercynian M. — R. Vistŭla. Viădus, *Oder.* Albis, *Elbe.* Rhenus, *Rhine.* — Saltus Teutoburgensis.† — Cimbric Chersonēsus, *Jutland.* — Ingævŏnes. Istævŏnes. Hermiŏnes. — Boii. Suevi. Cherusci.

**Britannia** or **Britain.** First invaded by Julius Cæsar, B. C. 55; conquered by Agricŏla, A. D. 84; abandoned by the Romans, A. D. 410. — Londinium. Verulamium, *St. Albans.* Eborăcum, *York.* — R. Tamĕsis, *Thames.* Sabrīna, *Severn.* Abus, *Humber.* — Pr. Cantium, *N. Foreland.* — Walls of Hadrian and Sevērus. — Id. Orcădes, *Orkney.* Mona, *Man.* Mona, *Anglesea.* Hibernia, *Ireland.* — Fretum Gallĭcum, *Str. of Dover.* — Oceanus Germanĭcus. — Trinobantes, *Essex.* Brigantes, *York.* Icēni, *Norfolk and Suffolk.* Silūres, *S. Wales.*

## XVIII.

### Gallia or Gaul. (Map 6.)

The southern part was made a Roman province, Narbonensis, 2d cent. B. C.; the rest was divided by Augustus, after the conquest by Cæsar, into three provinces, Aquitania, Lugdunensis, Belgĭca.

Lugdūnum, *Lyons.* Massilia, *Marseilles.* Narbo, *Narbonne.* Aquæ Sextiæ,† *Aix.* Tolōsa, *Toulouse.* Lutetia, *Paris.* Colonia Agrippīna, *Cologne.* Nemausus, *Nismes.*

M. Jura. Vosēgus, *Vosges.* Cebenna, *Cevennes.*

R. Mosella, *Moselle.* Mosa, *Meuse.* Scaldis, *Scheldt.* Sequāna, *Seine.* Matrŏna, *Marne.* Liger, *Loire.* Garumna, *Garonne.* Rhodănus, *Rhone.* Arar, *Saone.*

L. Lemānus, *Geneva.*

Armorĭca, *Brittany and Normandy.* — Allobrŏges, *Viennois.* Arverni, *Auvergne.* Ædui, *Burgundy.* Helvetii, *Switzerland.* Sequăni, *Franche Comté.* Remi, *Champagne.* Nervii, *Flanders.*

## XIX.

### Hispania. (Map 7.)

Conquered by the Romans from the Carthaginians, and made into two provinces, Citerior or Tarraconensis, and Ulterior or Bætĭca, B. C. 205. Lusitania, *Portugal,* made a province by Augustus.

Tarrăco, *Tarragōna.* Saguntum. Carthāgo Nova, *Cartagena.* Numantia. Gades, *Cadiz.* Munda.† Cordŭba, *Cordova.*

M. Pyrenæi.

R. Ibērus, *Ebro.* Durius, *Douro.* Tagus. Anas, *Guadiana.* Baetis, *Guadalquivir.*

Cantabri. Celtibēri. Ilergētes. Turdetāni.

Oceănus Cantabrĭcus, *B. of Biscay.* Mare Atlanticum. Mare Intērnum, *Mediterranean S.*

## XX.

### Italy I. (Map 8.)

**Liguria.** — Graian Alps. — Sinus Ligustĭcus, *G. of Genoa.* — Alpes Maritĭmæ made a Roman province by Augustus, Alpes Cottiæ by Nero, Alpes Pennīnæ later.

**Gallia Cisalpina,** *Lombardy, Emilia, &c.* Made into a

# ANCIENT GEOGRAPHY. 21

Roman province [acc. to Mommsen] by Sulla. Mediolānum, *Milan*. Placentia, *Piacenza*. Brixia, *Brescia*. Cremōna. Mantua. Mutīna, *Módena*. Bononia, *Bologna*. Ravenna. Vercellæ.† (Campi Raudii.) — Lepontine Alps. — R. Padus, *Po*. Ticīnus,† *Ticíno*. Trebia.† Athĕsis, *Ad'ige*. Rubĭcon. — L. Verbānus, *Maggiore*. Larius, *Como*. Benācus, *Garda*. — Lingŏnes. Cenomāni. Insūbres. Boii. Senŏnes. — Via Æmilia. **Venetia.** — Verōna. Patavium, *Padua*. Adria. Aquileia. — Carnic, Julian Alps. — Tergestīnus Sinus, *G. of Trieste*. — Istria.

## XXI.
### ITALY II. (Maps 8 and 9.)

**Etruria,** *Tuscany, &c.* A confederacy of twelve aristocratic cities; at the height of its power about B. C. 500. Afterwards subdued by Rome. — Pisæ. Fæsŭlæ,† *Fiésole*. Florentia, *Florence*. Arretium, *Arezzo*. Cortōna. Perusia, *Perugia*. Clusium, *Chiusi*. Falerii, *Civita Castellana*. Veii. Tarquinii. Agylla or Cære. — M. Apennīnus. Soracte. — R. Arnus. Tibĕr. — L. Trasimēnus.† Vulsiniensis. — Via Flaminia. Cassia. Aurelia.

**Umbria.** — Ariminum, *Rimini*. Sentīnum.† Spoletium, *Spoléto*. — R. Metaurus.† Nar.

**Picenum.** — Ancōna. Hadria.

**Sabinum.** The tribes contended with Rome in the Social War, B. C. 90. — Reāte. Amitērnum. Cures. Fidēnæ. Corfinium or Italia. Alba Fucensis. — M. Lucretīlis. Sacer. — R. Allia.† — L. Fucīnus. — Marsi. Pæligni. Vestīni. Marrucīni.

## XXII.

### Italy III. (Maps 9 and 11.)

**Latium.** A confederacy of thirty towns, with Alba Longa at the head. Rome supplanted Alba Longa, and obtained the mastery over Latium, 4th cent. B. C. — Rome. Ostia. Laurentum. Ardea. Antium. Anxur or Tarracīna. Coriŏli. Alba Longa. Gabii. Lanuvium. Aricia. Tuscŭlum, *Frascáti.* Præneste, *Palestrína.* Tibur, *Tívoli.* Formiæ, *Mola di Gáeta.* Anagnia. Fregellæ.—M. Albānus. — R. Liris, *Garigliáno.* Anio. Trerus. — L. Albānus. Regillus.† — Pr. Circeium. — Mulvian Bridge.† — Via Appia. Latīna. Valeria. — Æqui. Volsci. Hernĭci.

**Samnium.** Waged war with Rome for more than fifty years in the 4th and 3d centuries B. C. — Boviānum. Beneventum.† — M. Taburnus. — R. Tifernus. — Caudine Forks.† — Frentani. Pentri. Hirpĭni.

**Apulia.** Mostly pasture lands. — Cannæ.† Brundusium. Lucerĭa. Canusium. — M. Gargānus. — R. Aufīdus. — Pr. Japygium. — Daunia. Calabria.

## XXIII.

### Italy IV. (Map 9.)

**Campania.** — Capua. Cumæ. Baiæ. Puteŏli, *Pozzuóli.* Neapŏlis or Parthenŏpe. Herculaneum. Pompeii. Nola. Teānum. — M. Massĭcus. Tifāta. Gaurus.† Vesuvius. — R. Vulturnus. — L. Avernus. Lucrīnus. — Pr. Misēnum. — Ager Falernus. — Mare Tyrrhēnum or Infĕrum. — Id. Ænaria or Pithecūsa, *Ischia.* Capreæ, *Capri.*

**Lucania.** Colonized by Sabines. — Potentia. — Sinus Tarentīnus.

**Bruttium.** A mixed people, made up of Lucanians, Œnotrians, and revolted slaves. — Pr. Lacinium. Leucopetra. Zephyrium.

**Magna Græcia.** (Greek Colonies.) — Tarentum. Metapontum. Heraclēa. Sybăris. Thurii. Croton. Locri Epizephyrii. Rhegium, *Reggio.* Pæstum. Velia or Elea.

## XXIV.

### ROME. (Map 10.)

**Seven Hills.** — Palatīnus. Capitolīnus. Quirinālis. Viminālis. Esquilīnus. Cælius. Aventīnus. — M. Janicŭlum.

**Forum** — Romānum. Boarium. Trajāni.

**Circus** — Maxĭmus. Flaminius.

**Baths** — of Titus, Caracalla, Diocletian.

**Temple** — of Jupiter Capitolīnus. Jupiter Stator. Saturn. Peace. Concord. Vesta. Castor and Pollux. Venus and Rome. — Panthĕon.

**Arch** — of Drusus, Titus, Septimius Severus, Constantine.

**Column** — of Trajan, M. Aurelius.

**Porta** — Capēna. Collīna.† Carmentālis.

Campus Martius. Ager Vaticānus. Prata Quinctia. Suburra. Velia. Arx. Tarpeian Rock. Agger. Tiber Island. Via Sacra. Clivus Capitolīnus. Vicus Tuscus.

Colossēum or Flavian Amphitheatre. Mausolēum of Hadrian, *Castle St. Angelo.* Theatre of Marcellus. Sublician Bridge. Claudian Aqueduct. Curia. Comitium. Tabularium. Mamertine Prison. Basilĭca of Constantine.

# THE ROMAN PROVINCES

### ARRANGED CHRONOLOGICALLY.

*∗* The Senatorial Provinces are distinguished by the asterisk; the rest are Imperial. (§ 154.) (Map 4.)

## TO THE REIGN OF AUGUSTUS.

| B. C. | | B. C. | |
|---|---|---|---|
| 241. | Sicilia.* | 30. | Ægyptus. |
| 238. | Sardinia. | 29. | Mœsia. |
| 205. | Hispania Citerior. | 27. | Aquitania. |
| 205. | "    Ulterior.* | 27. | Lugdunensis. |
| 167. | Illyrĭcum (Dalmatia). | 27. | Belgĭca. |
| 146. | Macedonia.* | 27 ? | Lusitania. |
| 146. | Achaia.* | 27 ? | Germania Superior. |
| 146. | Afrĭca.* | 27 ? | Germania Inferior. |
| 129. | Asia.* | 27. | Cyprus.* |
| 120. | Gallia Narbonensis.* | 25. | Galatia. |
| 82 ? | Gallia Cisalpīna (until 43). | 25. | Pamphylia et Lycia (A.D.43). |
| 74. | Bithynia.* | 15. | Rhætia. |
| 74. | Cyrēne et Creta (67).* | 15. | Norĭcum. |
| 64. | Cilicia. | 14. | Alpes Maritĭmæ. |
| 64. | Syria. | A D. 8. | Pannonia. |

## AFTER AUGUSTUS.

| A. D. | | A. D. | |
|---|---|---|---|
| 17. | Cappadocia. | 63. | Pontus Polemoniăcus. |
| 39. | Numidia. | 73. | Commagēne. |
| 42. | Mauretania Tingitāna. | —. | Epīrus (by Trajan). |
| 42. | Mauretania Cæsariensis. | 105. | Arabia. |
| 43. | Britannia. | 106. | Dacia. |
| 46. | Thracia. | —. | Alpes Pennīnæ (before Aurelian). |
| —. | Alpes Cottiæ (by Nero). | | |

Armenia, Mesopotamia, and Assyria were made provinces by Trajan, but immediately given up.

# ANCIENT CHRONOLOGY.

In these tables, those nations which successively held the chief place in the world's history are taken in turn as representatives each of its period, the dates of primary importance being indicated by full-faced type, and the contemporary events of other countries by italics. In this way synchronism is preserved, without the confusion of parallel columns, and, above all, prominence is given to what properly belongs to Universal History, and to the course of empire. There are in strictness three such periods, — Oriental, Grecian, and Roman, — but for convenience' sake the Roman Empire is considered as a fourth. Grote has been the authority in Grecian dates, Mommsen in Roman, Bunsen in Egyptian; in other cases we have followed the best authorities within our reach. The dagger (†) indicates a battle.

On the opposite pages are placed the names of writers, artists, &c., as nearly as possible opposite the period at which they flourished. The letter L. signifies Latin writers; Ch., Christian fathers.

# 1.

## ORIENTAL PERIOD,

EXTENDING to about B. C. 500, and comprising in succession the **Egyptian, Assyrian, Ninevite, Babylonian,** and **Persian** Empires. In this period the Greek states were wholly disunited politically, Sparta being the most powerful. The Roman monarchy falls entirely within this period.

### EGYPTIAN EMPIRE.

B. C.
3619. Menes, the first king.
    Fourth Dynasty in Memphis. (Pyramids.)
    Twelfth Dynasty in Diospŏlis, or Thebes. (Lake Mœris.)
    Hycsos or Shepherd Kings.
    [Chaldæan Empire in Babylon.]
1625. Eighteenth Dynasty in Thebes. — 1540. Thothmes III.
1409. Nineteenth Dynasty. Ramĕses II. (Sesostris). Height of Egyptian power.
1314. Exodus of the Israelites under Moses. (K. Menephthah.)

1273. ASSYRIAN EMPIRE.
    [Kingdoms of Jerusalem, Tyre, and Damascus.]
1184. *Troy taken by the Greeks, after a siege of ten years.*
1104. *Return of the Heraclidæ. — Doric Kingdoms in the Peloponnēsus.*
985. Revolt of the Ten Tribes. — Kingdoms of Israel and Judah.
817. *Legislation of Lycurgus in Sparta.*

---

**David,** the Hebrew psalmist, lived in the 11th cent.; **Homer** is sometimes placed as early, by Grote as late as 850; **Hesiod** lived not far from 800; also the prophet *Joel*.

**776.** *First Olympiad. Commencement of Greek Chronology.*
**753.** *Assumed date of the building of Rome. Roman Chronology.*
**747.** **Era of Nabonassar.** — Assyrian Empire of Nineveh.
**743.** *First Messenian War; — conquest of Messenia by Sparta.*
**721.** Samaria taken by the Assyrians. (K. Sargon.)
**664.** Twenty-sixth Egyptian Dynasty, founded by Psammetĭchus.
**648.** *Second Messenian War. (Aristomĕnes.)*
  [Kingdoms of Media and Lydia.]
**625.** **Nineveh destroyed** by Medes and Babylonians.

" EMPIRE OF BABYLON.
**624.** *Legislation of Draco in Athens.*
**594.** *Legislation of Solon in Athens.* T i m o c r a c y *established* (§ 91).
**586.** Jerusalem taken by Nebuchadnezzar, K. of Babylon.
**560.** *Tyranny of Pisistrătus in Athens.*

**559.** PERSIAN EMPIRE.
**546.** Conquest of Lydia (K. Crœsus) by Cyrus, K. of Persia.
**538.** **Babylon taken** by Cyrus.
**536.** Return of the Jews from captivity [70 years] in Babylon.
**525.** Conquest of Egypt by Cambȳses. Pelusium.†
**510.** *The Pisistratīdæ expelled from Athens.* D e m o c r a c y established by Clisthĕnes (§ 92).
**509.** *Expulsion of the Tarquins by Brutus. Roman Republic.*

## LITERATURE AND ART.    29

The Israelite prophets, *Amos* and *Hosea.*

The Hebrew prophets, **Isaiah** and *Micah.*

The I a m b i c poets: **Archilochus** of Paros, and *Simonĭdes* of Amorgos. — The E l e g í a c poets: *Callinus* of Ephĕsus, and **Tyrtæus** (2d Messenian War). — *Terpander* of Lesbos, inventor of the seven-stringed lyre. — *Alcman* of Sardes, c h o r i c poet.

The Hebrew prophets, *Nahum* and *Zephaniah.*

*Epimenĭdes,* the Cretan philosopher.

*Arīon* of Lesbos, inventor of the D i t h y r a m b. — L y r i c poets: **Alcæus** and **Sappho** of Lesbos, and *Stesichŏrus* of Himĕra. — *Mimnermus* of Colŏphon. — *Æsop* the fabulist.

The Hebrew prophets, *Habakkuk,* **Jeremiah,** *Obadiah,* and **Ezekiel.**

Poets: **Anacreon** of Teos, *Theognis* of Megăra, *Hippōnax* of Ephĕsus.

535. First representation of Tragedy by *Thespis.*

### Greek Philosophy.

*Anaximander* of Milētus, of the IONIC School.

X e n o p h a n e s of Colŏphon, founder of the ELEATIC School.

P y t h a g ŏ r a s of Samos, founder of the PYTHAGORÉAN School.

---

### THE SEVEN WISE MEN OF GREECE.

About B. C. 600. — **Solon** of Athens, **Thales** of Milētus (founder of the Ionic School of philosophy), *Pittăcus* of Mytilēne, *Bias* of Priēne, *Cleobūlus* of Lindus, *Myson* of Chenæ, and *Chilon* of Sparta. — Some lists contained *Periander* of Corinth instead of Myson.

## II.

### GRECIAN PERIOD.

From about B. C. 500 to 300; the Hegem'ony or leadership successively held by **Athens, Sparta, Thebes,** and **Macedonia.** During this period the Persian empire continued in the East, constantly waning in power until overthrown by Alexander. Roman history is divided into two lesser periods: — 1. The struggles between the Patricians and Plebeians, terminated by the Licinian Laws. 2. The conquest of Italy, completed in the battle of Sentīnum.

502. Ionic Revolt from Persia. Suppressed at Id. Lade,† 496.
498. *L. Regillus.*† *Independence of the Roman Republic established.*
494. *First Secession of the Plebs to the Sacred Mount.*
**490.** **Invasion of Greece by Darius. Marathon.**† (Miltiădes.)
**480.** **Invasion by Xerxes. Thermopylæ.**† — Artemisium.†
" Salămis'.† Naval victory of Themistocles.
" Himĕra.† Carthaginians defeated by Gelon.
479. **Platæa.**† (Aristīdes and Pausanias.) — Mycălc† (same day).
 Career of Themistocles (*d.* about 449).
476. Confederacy of Delos. — ATHENIAN HEGEMONY.
467. Revolt of Naxos from Athens.
466. R. Eurymĕdon.† Defeat of the Persians by Cimon.
464. Revolt of the Messenians from Sparta: subdued, 455.
 *Wars of Rome with the Æquians and Volscians.*
 Athenian Empire.
451. *Legislation of the Decemvirs in Rome.*
446. Coronēa.† The Athenians defeated by the Bœotians.
 Age of Pericles (*d.* 429).
**431.** **Peloponnesian War,** between Athens and Sparta, — ends 404.
425. Id. Sphacteria.† Victory of the Athenians under Cleon.

# LITERATURE AND ART.

*Heraclĭtus* of Ephĕsus the "Weeping Philosopher."

**Simonides** of Ceos, Lyric Poet. 556 – 469.

**Aeschylus**, Tragic Poet, 525 – 456. [First Victory, 484.]

**Pindar**, the greatest of lyric poets, d. 442.

**Anaxagoras** of Clazomĕnæ, founder of the ATTIC School of Philosophy.

**Sophocles**, Tragic Poet, 495 – 406. [Victory over Æschylus, 468.]

**Euripides**, last of the three great Tragic Poets, 480 – 406.

*Empedocles* of Agrigentum, statesman and philosopher.

**Herodotus** of Halicarnassus, "Father of History," d. 484.

*Polygnōtus* of Thasos, painter.
**Phidias**, the greatest of sculptors.
*Ictīnus*, architect of the Parthĕnon [finished 438].
Sculptors: *Polyclētus*, founder of the Argive School, and *Myron*.

## ANCIENT CHRONOLOGY.

421. Fifty years' truce agreed upon — broken, 415.
415. Disastrous Athenian expedition to Syracuse.† (Nicias.)
    Career of Alcibiades.
406. Dionysius the Elder, Tyrant at Syracuse.
**405.** **Aegospotami.**† (Lysander.) — SPARTAN HEGEMONY.
403. Athenian independence re-established by Thrasybūlus.
401. Expedition [Anabăsis] of Cyrus the Younger. — Cunaxa.†
396. *Veii taken by Camillus, after a siege of ten years.*
394. Cnidus.†  Naval power of Sparta destroyed by Conon.
 "  Coronēa.†  The Bœotians defeated by Agesilāus, K. of Sparta.
**390.** *R. Allia.*†  *Capture of Rome by the Gauls.*
387. Peace of Antalcĭdas between Greece and Persia.
**371.** **Leuctra.**†  Spartan power broken. — THEBAN HEGEMONY.
    Career of Epaminondas.
367. *Licinian laws in Rome. Equality of the orders.*
364. Pelopĭdas of Thebes slain in battle with Alexander of Pheræ.
362. Mantinēa.†  Death of Epaminondas.
355. Phocian or Sacred War, until 346.
    Career of Demosthenes (*d.* 322).
348. Olynthus taken by Philip of Macedon.
344. Timoleon becomes master of Syracuse, *d.* 336.
    *First Samnite War.* — 343. *Mt. Gaurus.*† — *Latin War.*
**338.** **Chæronea** † (Philip). — MACEDONIAN HEGEMONY.
334. Expedition of Alexander. — R. Granīcus.†
333. Issus.† — 332. Capture of Tyre.
**331.** **Gaugamela** (Arbēla).†  Overthrow of the Persian Empire.

### MACEDONIAN EMPIRE.

323. Death of Alexander: dismemberment of the Empire.
    *Second Samnite War.* — 321. *Caudine Forks.*†
301. Ipsus.†  Overthrow of the Asiatic kingdom of Antigŏnus.
    [Kingdoms of Macedonia, Syria, and Egypt.]
    *Third Samnite War.*  295. *Sentīnum.*†  290. *Peace.*
[Rise of the Achæan and Ætolian Leagues.]

## LITERATURE AND ART.

*Apollodōrus* of Athens, founder of a school of painting.
**Thucydides**, the greatest of ancient historians, *b.* 471.
**Zeuxis** and **Parrhasius**, painters.
**Socrates**, the philosopher; condemned to death 399, æt. 70.

**Aristophanes**, the comic poet; about 444 – 380.
*Lysias*, the Athenian orator, 458 – 378.
*Democrĭtus* of Abdēra, the "Laughing Philosopher," 460 – 357.
**Plato**, founder of the Academic School of Philosophy, ℣. 430.
*Hippocrătes*, founder of the science of medicine, *d.* 357.
*Antisthĕnes*, founder of the Cynic School of Philosophy.
Later Attic school of sculpture: *Scopas* and **Praxiteles**.
**Xenophon** the historian, *d.* 359.
**Isocrates**, founder of a school of oratory, 436 – 338.
**Aristotle**, founder of the Peripatetic School of Philosophy, 384 – 322.
Orations of **Demosthenes** (*b.* 385): — 351, 1st Philippic. 349, Olynthiacs. 346, On the Peace. 343, 2d Philippic. 341, 3d Philippic.
**Apelles** of Cos, the painter.
*Lysippus* of Sicyon, sculptor of the school of Polyclētus.
**Diogenes**, the Cynic Philosopher, *d.* 323.
*Æschĭnes*, the orator, 389 – 314.
*Menander*, the most distinguished poet of the New Comedy, *b.* 342.
330. Oration of *Demosthĕnes* on the Crown.
**Euclid**, the mathematician, *d.* 283.
*Theophrastus*, pupil of Aristotle, 374 – 287.

### Schools of Philosophy.

*Pyrrho*, founder of the Sceptic School, *d.* 288.
**Zeno**, founder of the Stoic School, *d.* 263.
**Epicurus**, founder of the Epicurēan School, *d.* 270.
*Arcesilāus*, founder of the Middle Academy.

## III.

## ROMAN PERIOD.

From about B. C. 300 to the Christian Era: divided into the periods of **Foreign Wars** and **Civil Dissensions**.

In the East the Diadŏchi, or Successors of Alexander, and the Parthian Empire. In Greece an attempt at confederation, in the Ætolian and Achæan leagues, then conquest by Rome.

### PERIOD OF FOREIGN WARS.

      Invasion of Italy by Pyrrhus; 275, defeated at Beneventum.†
- **264.** **First Punic War** — For the possession of Sicily.
- 260. Naval victory of Duilius, near Messāna.
- 255. Defeat and captivity of Regŭlus.
- 241. Id. Ægātes.† Victory of Catŭlus. — Peace made.
      [*Parthian Empire and Kingdom of Pergămum.*]
- 222. *Sellasia*.† *Supremacy of the Achæan League in the Peloponnēsus.*
- **219.** Siege of Saguntum, by Hannĭbal. — **Second Punic War.**
- 218. Victories of Hannĭbal at R. Ticīnus † and R. Trebia.†
- 217. L. Trasimēnus.† — 216. **Cannæ.**†
- 212. Syracuse taken by Marcellus. Death of Archimēdes.
- 207. R. Metaurus.† Defeat of Hasdrŭbal by Livius and Nero.
- **202.** **Zama.**† Defeat of Hannĭbal by Scipio Africānus. Peace.
- 197. Cynoscephălæ.† Defeat of Philip of Macĕdon by Flamininus.
- 190. Magnesia.† Defeat of Antiŏchus of Syria by Scipio Asiatĭcus.
- 183. Death of Scipio Africānus, Hannĭbal, and Philopœmen.
- 168. Pydna.† Defeat of Perseus of Macĕdon by L. Æmilius Paulus. End of Third Macedonian War.
- 149. Revolt of Viriāthus in Spain.
- **146.** **Corinth taken by Mummius, Carthage by Scipio Aemilianus.**

Alexandrian School
of Literature, under the patronage of Ptolemy Philadelphus.
*Aristarchus* of Samos, astronomer.
*Lycŏphron*, grammarian and poet, famed for obscurity.
**Theocritus** of Syracuse, and *Bion* of Smyrna, pastoral poets.
*Manĕtho*, the Egyptian historian.
**Callimachus**, the greatest of the Alexandrian poets, *d*. abt. 240.
240. First play exhibited at Rome by *Livius Andronĭcus*. L.
**Archimedes** of Syracuse, mechanical philosopher, 287 – 212.
**Eratosthenes**, the first mathematical geographer, 276 – abt. 196.
*Moschus* of Syracuse, pastoral poet.
*Cn. Nævius*, the earliest native Roman poet. L.
**Aristarchus** of Alexandrīa, critic and grammarian.
**Plautus**, the earliest Roman comedian, *d*. 184. L.
*Ennius*, epic and tragic poet, a Greek by birth, 239 – abt. 167. L.
*Q. Fabius Pictor*, the earliest Roman historian, wrote in Greek.
*Apollonius Rhodius*, Alexandrian poet, *b*. abt. 235.
**M. Porcius Cato** Major, the Censor; historian, abt. 234 – 149. L.
*Carneădes*, founder of the NEW ACADEMY, abt. 213 – 129.
*Pacuvius* and *Attius*, tragedians.
**Terence**, the Roman comedian, *b*. at Carthage, 195. L.
**Hipparchus** of Alexandrīa, the greatest of ancient astronomers.
**Polybius**, the Greek historian of Rome, abt. 204 – 122.

## PERIOD OF CIVIL DISSENSIONS.

- **133.** **Legislation of Ti. Gracchus.** — Numantia taken by Scipio.
- 132. Servile insurrection in Sicily (headed by Eunus) suppressed.
- 121. Legislation and death of C. Gracchus. Aristocratic reaction.
- 106. War with Jugurtha finished by Marius.
- 102. Aquæ Sextiæ.† Teutones defeated by Marius.
- 101. Campi Raudii.† Cimbri defeated by Marius.
- 100. End of second servile war in Sicily. (Athenion.)
- 90. Social or Marsic War. Ended, 88.
- **88.** **Civil War between Marius and Sulla.**
- " War against Mithridates in Asia (Sulla) : ended, 63.
- 87. Victory of Marius and Cinna. — Massacre of the party of Sulla.
- 82. Colline Gate.† — Dictatorship and legislation of Sulla.
- 78. Death of Sulla. — Civil War between Catulus and Lepidus.
- " Sertorius continues the war in Spain : murdered, 72.
- 73. Insurrection of Spartacus; suppressed, 71, by Crassus.
- " Lucullus conducts the Mithridatic War successfully.
- 67. Pompey subdues the pirates, and takes command against Mithridates. — 63. Death of Mithridates.
- **63.** Cicero consul. — **Conspiracy of Catiline.**
- **60.** **First Triumvirate, of Cæsar, Pompey, and Crassus.**
- 58. Cæsar takes command in Gaul; completes its conquest, 51.
- 53. Carrhæ.† Crassus defeated and killed by the Parthians.
- **49.** **Civil War between Cæsar and Pompey.**
- 48. Pharsalus.† Pompey defeated, and afterwards murdered.
- 47. Zela.† Defeat of Pharnaces. "Veni, vidi, vici."
- 46. Thapsus.† Defeat of Pompey's party. Cato the Younger kills himself at Utica.
- 45. Munda.† The sons of Pompey defeated by Cæsar.
- **44.** **Assassination of Cæsar,** by Brutus and Cassius.
- 43. Second Triumvirate, of Octavianus, Antony, and Lepidus.
- 42. Philippi.† Brutus and Cassius defeated by the Triumvirs.
- **31.** **Actium.**† Antony defeated by Octavianus.

*Lucilius*, founder of Roman satire, d. 103. L.

*L. Crassus*, b. 140: *M. Antonius*, b. 143, distinguished orators. L.

81. Earliest extant Oration of Cicero, *Pro Quinctio.*
*Q. Hortensius*, orator, rival of Cicero, b. 114. L.

**M. Tullius Cicero,** 106 – 43. L.
70. Orations of **Cicero,** *In Verrem;* 66, *Pro Lege Manilia,* and *Pro Cluentio.*
*T. Lucretius Carus*, philosophical poet, 95 – abt. 52. L.
*Q. Roscius*, the great comic actor, d. 62. L.
63. Orations, *De Lege Agraria, In Catilinam, Pro Murēna,* &c. L.
*M. Terentius Varro*, writer on Agriculture and Antiquities, 116 – 28. L.
**Catullus,** lyric poet, b. 87. L.
52. Oration of Cicero, *Pro Milōne.* L.
**C. Sallustius Crispus,** the historian, 86 – 34. L.
**C. Julius Cæsar,** historian and orator, 100 – 44. L.
Orations of Cicero: 47, *Pro Marcello;* 46, *Pro Ligario;* 45, *Pro Deiotăro.*

44. First two *Philippics* of Cicero against Mark Antony.
43. Twelve Philippics of Cicero against Antony.

*Verrius Flaccus*, antiquarian. — *Trogus Pompeius*, historian.

## IV.

### ROMAN EMPIRE.

From near the Christian era, lasting about 500 years. In the East the Parthian empire, until overthrown by the new Persian empire.

B.C. 30. Octaviānus AUGUSTUS. First Roman Emperor — Second Cæsar.
    12. Death of Agrippa, chief minister of Augustus.
    9. Saltus Teutoburgensis.† Varus defeated by Arminius.
A.D. 14. TIBERIUS. — 19. Death of Germanicus in Syria.
    31. Execution of Sejānus, the Emperor's favorite.
    37. CALIGŪLA.
    41. CLAUDIUS. — 50. Invasion of Britain (Caractăcus).
    54. NERO. — Last Emperor of the **Claudian** House.
    61. Insurrection in Britain (Boadicēa).
    64. Fire in Rome. Persecution of the Christians.
    68. GALBA. — 69. OTHO. — VITELLIUS.
    69. VESPASIAN. — **Flavian** House, of three Emperors.
    **70.** Jerusalem taken by Titus, after siege of five months.
    78. Agricŏla takes the command in Britain. Recalled, 85.
    79. TITUS. — Destruction of Herculaneum and Pompeii.
    81. DOMITIAN. — Last of the Twelve Cæsars.
    96. NERVA. — First of the Five Good Emperors.
    **98.** TRAJAN. — The Roman Empire at its height.
    106. Dacia made a Roman province.
    117. HADRIAN. — A patron of the arts.
    138. ANTONĪNUS PIUS.
    161. MARCUS AURELIUS, the Philosopher.
    180. COMMŎDUS. — The Empire ruled by the Prætorian Guard.
    193. PERTĬNAX. — DIDIUS JULIANUS.
    " SEPTIMIUS SEVERUS. — House of the **Severi**.

Augustan or Golden Age of Roman Literature. — **C. Cilnius Mæcenas**, *d.* 8., æt. abt. 60.

Latin Poets — Epic, **Virgil**, 70 - 19. — Lyric and Satiric, **Horace**, 65 - 8. — Elegiac, **Tibullus**, *b.* abt. 54; *Propertius, b.* abt. 57. — **Ovid**, 43 - A. D. 18. — Historians — **Livy**, 59 - A. D. 17. — *Cornelius Nepos.*

Greek Historians — *Dionysius Halicarnassensis; d.* abt. B. C. 7 : *Diodōrus Sicŭlus. — Strabo,* geographer.

*Philo the Jew*, the Alexandrian Platonist.

*Celsus*, medical writer. L. — *Valerius Maxĭmus* and *Velleius Patercŭlus,* historians. L.

*Columella*, on Agriculture. L. — *Vitruvius*, on Architecture. L.

*Lucan*, epic poet, author of *Pharsalia*, 39 - 65. L.

*Senĕca*, moral philosopher and tragedian, *d.* 65. L.

*Persius*, the satirist, 34 - 62. L. — *Phædrus*, the fabulist (uncertain). L.

*Silius Italĭcus*, epic poet, author of *Punĭca*, 25 - 100. L.

*Q. Curtius*, life of Alexander, time unknown. L.

**Pliny** the Elder, naturalist, 23 - 79. L.

Epic Poets — *Valerius Flaccus, d.* 88. — *Statius,* abt. 61 - 96. L.

*Flavius Josēphus*, the Jewish historian. 37 - abt. 100.

**Quintilian**, the rhetorician, abt. 40 - 118. — *Frontĭnus, d* abt. 106. L.

**Juvenal** the satirist. L. — *Martial* the epigrammatist, 43 - abt. 104. L.

Ignatius, of Antioch, martyred abt. 107. Ch.

**Tacitus**, the historian. L. — *Pliny* the Younger, *b.* abt. 61. L.

**Plutarch** and *Suetonius* (L.), biographers. — *Pausanias*, the traveller. — **Ptolemy**, the geographer. — *Lucian*, the Satirist. — *Fronto*, orator. L.

*Justin Martyr.* Ch. — *Polycarp*, Bishop of Smyrna. Ch.

*Appuleius*, author of "The Golden Ass." — *Gaius*, jurist. L.

*Irenæus*, Bishop of Lyons. Ch. — *Marcion*, a heretic. Ch.

*Galen*, medical writer, *d.* about 200. L. — *Athenæus.*

211. CARACALLA. — 218. ELAGABALUS.
222. ALEXANDER SEVERUS, murdered by MAXIMĪNUS.
226. *Parthian Empire overthrown. New Persian Empire of the Sassanĭdæ.*
Invasions of the Empire by Goths, Franks, &c.
260. The Emperor Valerian made prisoner by Sapor of Persia.
The Thirty Tyrants — rebels in various parts of the Empire.
273. Palmȳra (Q. Zenobia) taken by Aurelian.
284. DIOCLETIAN. — 303. Tenth Persecution of the Christians.
**306.** CONSTANTINE.
312. Mulvian Bridge † Authority of Constantine established.
Christianity made the State Religion.
325. First General Council of the Church at Nicæa (*Nice*).
330. Constantinople made the capital of the Empire.
361. JULIAN the Apostate.
379. THEODOSIUS the Great.
395. Division of the Empire: the East under ARCADIUS; the West under HONORIUS.
**410.** **Rome sacked by Al'aric the Visigoth.**
" Britain abandoned by the Romans.
415. Visigothic Kingdom in Spain founded by Ataulphus.
429. Vandal Kingdom of **Gen'seric** in North Africa.
449. Britain conquered by the Anglo-Saxons.
451. "Battle of the Peoples." — Defeat of **Attila** the Hun by Theod'oric the Visigoth, and Aëtius.
**476.** **Roman Empire overthrown by Odoacer.**
481. Clovis, founder of the French monarchy, d. 511.
493. Theod'oric the Great, founder of the Empire of the Ostrogoths, d. 526.

*Clement* of Alexandria, abt. 193–217.  Ch.
**Tertullian** of Carthage, *d.* 220.  L. Ch.
*Cassius Dio*, the historian.
**Origen** of Alexandria, 185–253.  Ch. — *Cyprian*, Bishop of Carthage, *d.* 258.  L. Ch.
**Longinus**, "On the Sublime," *d.* 273.
*Plotinus*, the mystic philosopher. — *Porphyry*, his disciple, an opponent of Christianity.

*Arnobius* and *Lactantius*.  L. Ch.
**Eusebius**, Bishop of Cæsarea, *d.* about 340.  Ch.
**Arius** of Alexandria, a heretic, *d.* 336.  Ch.
**Athanasius**, Archbishop of Alexandria, *d.* 373.  Ch.
*Ammiānus Marcellīnus*, a Greek historian, *d.* about 390.  L.
**Basil**, Bishop of Cæsarea, renowned for eloquence, 329–379.  Ch.
**Gregory Nazianzen**, Patriarch of Constantinople, 329–390.  Ch.
**Ambrose**, Bishop of Milan, 340–397.  L. Ch.
**Chrysostom**, Archbishop of Constantinople, 347–407.  Ch.
*Claudian*, the last Roman poet.  L.
**Jerome** (*Hieronymus*), *b.* at Stridon 331, *d.* 420.  L. Ch.
*Pelagius*, a heretic.  L. Ch.
**Augustine**, Bishop of Hippo, 354–330.  L. Ch.
**Cyril**, Archbishop of Alexandria, *d.* 444.  Ch.


*Boëtius*, Roman philosopher, about 470–524.  L.

# OUTLINES OF ANCIENT CHRONOLOGY

## BY CENTURIES.

Cent.
B. C.

6th. Persian Empire. — Tyranny of Pisistrătus. — Roman Monarchy. Solon. Cyrus. Pythagŏras.

### Grecian Period.

5th. Persian Invasion. — Athenian Hegemony. — Peloponnesian War. — Roman Republic. — Struggles of Patricians and Plebeians. Themistocles. Æschȳlus. Pericles. Phidias. Socrătes.

4th. Spartan and Theban Hegemonies. — Macedonian Empire. Samnite Wars. — Roman Conquest of Italy.
Plato. Epaminondas. Demosthĕnes. Aristotle. Alexander. Camillus. Appius Claudius Cœcus.

### Roman Period.

3d. Invasion of Pyrrhus. — First and Second Punic Wars. — The successors of Alexander. — Ætolian and Achæan Leagues. Dentātus. Hannibal. Scipio Africānus. Archimēdes.

2d. Conquest of Greece, &c. — Decay of the Republic.
Philopœmen. Cato the Censor. The Gracchi. Marius.

1st. Civil Wars. — Overthrow of the Republic.
Sulla. Cicero. Pompey. Cæsar. Virgil. Augustus.

### Roman Empire.

A. D.

1st. The Claudian and Flavian Houses. (The Twelve Cæsars.)

2d. The Empire at its height. — The Antonines. — Military despotism.

3d. A succession of worthless Emperors until Diocletian.

4th. A strong empire established by Constantine. — Christianity the state religion. — Division of the Empire.

5th. Invasions of the barbarians. — The Western Empire broken up. Alaric. Genseric. Attila. Odoăcer. Theodoric.

# MYTHOLOGY.

# GRECIAN MYTHOLOGY.

1. THE children of **Uranus**, *Heaven*, and **Gaia**, *Earth*, were the twelve Titans, among them Oceănus, Hyperion, Iapĕtus, Cronos, Rhea, Themis, and Mnemosўne; also the three Cyclops, and the three Hundred-handed, 'Εκατογχείρες, of whom Briareus was the most noted. Uranus was dethroned by **Cronos**, who married **Rhea** (§ 25), and was father of Zeus (§ 2), Hera (§ 3), Poseidon (§ 20), Hades (§ 29), and Hestia (§ 11). Cronos, in his turn, was dethroned by his sons, who then divided his realms, Zeus obtaining Heaven, Poseidon the Sea, and Hades the Infernal Regions. The Titans rebelled against Zeus, and attempted to scale heaven by piling Mt. Pelion upon Ossa, but were subdued with the aid of the Hundred-handed.

## I. HEAVEN (OLYMPIAN GODS).

2. **Zeus**, *Jupiter.*\* He was attended by the eagle, and wielded the thunderbolt. His most famous temple, and statue by Phidias, were at Olympia; his oracle, at Do-

\* The names of the Roman gods with whom these are usually identified are appended.

dōna; he was worshipped with peculiar rites and human sacrifices on Mt. Lycæus; also worshipped at Crete.

3. **Hera,** *Juno,* the goddess of marriage; especially worshipped at Samos and Argos; the peacock was sacred to her. Her statue by Polyclētus was at the Heræum, near Argos.

4. **Hephæstus,** *Vulcan,* god of fire; son of Zeus and Hera; lame, married to Aphrodīte; worshipped at Lemnos.

5. **Athena,** or **Pallas,** *Minerva,* goddess of wisdom, sprung from the head of Zeus: the patron deity of Athens, where her bronze statue, by Phidias, *Athēna Promăchos,* perhaps 70 feet high, stood on the Acropolis. Represented with helmet, shield, spear, the ægis, (a mantle on which is a gorgon's head, § 36,) and sometimes a serpent at her feet: the owl was sacred to her.

6. **Apollo,** or **Phœbus,** god of the sun and of art, son of Zeus and Leto, *Latōna.* Worshipped at Delos and Amÿclæ; his oracle was at Delphi, where he killed the serpent Python, and Mt. Parnassus was sacred to him. Represented with bow and arrows or a lyre. He drove the chariot of the sun about the earth daily, but one day permitted his son Phaëthon to take his place, who threw all things into confusion, and was struck down by a thunderbolt of Zeus. He killed his friend Hyacinthus by accident with a quoit, in whose honor the festival Hyacinthia (§ 116) was celebrated. He loved Daphne, who was changed into a laurel.

7. **Artemis,** or **Phœbe,** *Diāna,* his sister; goddess of the moon, of hunting, and chastity; worshipped at Delos,

Brauron, the Tauric Chersonēsus, and Ephĕsus: in love with Endymion, a beautiful youth represented in a perpetual sleep. She appears also as Hecate, a mysterious threefold being, representing sun, moon, and earth.

8. **Ares,** *Mars,* god of war, son of Zeus and Hera.

9. **Aphrodite,** *Venus,* goddess of beauty and love; sprung from the foam on the sea; worshipped at Corinth, Cyprus, and Cythēra. Her *cestus,* or girdle, conferred the power of fascination. She loved Adōnis, who was killed by a wild boar. — Eros, *Cupid,* son of Ares and Aphrodite: represented as a winged boy, with bow and arrows; in love with Psyche.

10. **Hermes,** *Mercury,* god of commerce, eloquence, and thieving, messenger of the gods; son of Zeus and Maia. He had a winged cap, wings on his feet, and carried a purse and the *caduceus,* a winged staff with two snakes coiled about it. He conducted the souls of the dead to the lower regions; hence called ψυχοπομπός.

11. **Hestia,** *Vesta,* goddess of the hearth.

## Lesser Deities of Heaven.

12. **Iris,** the *rainbow,* messenger between Heaven and Earth. — **Hebe,** *Youth,* the cup-bearer of the gods; her place was afterwards taken by Ganymede. — **Nike,** *Victory,* with palm and wreath; daughter of Zeus and Styx.

13. The **Hours,** Ὧραι, Eunomia, *Order,* Dike, *Right,* and Irēne, *Peace :* daughters of Zeus and Themis, *Justice* (§ 1). — Astræa was another daughter, who lived among men during the golden age, then withdrew among the stars.

14. The **Graces,** Χάριτες, Aglaia, Euphrosӯne, and Thalīa, daughters of Zeus and Eurynŏme.

15. The **Muses,** daughters of Zeus and Mnemosӯne (§ 1): they dwelt on Mt. Helicon, where were the fountains of Aganippe and Hippocrene. They were,— 1. **Clio,** of history, with a scroll.  2. **Calliope,** of epic poetry, with tablets and stylus.  3. **Euterpe,** of lyric poetry, with a double flute.  4. **Melpomene,** of tragedy, with a tragic mask, the club of Hercules, and the *cothurnus,* or buskin.  5. **Thalia,** of comedy, with a comic mask, a shepherd's staff, and wreath of ivy.  6. **Terpsichore,** of dancing, with lyre and *plectrum* (instrument for touching the strings of the lyre).  7. **Erato,** of amatory poetry, sometimes with the lyre.  8. **Polyhymnia,** of sacred song, veiled.  9. **Urania,** of astronomy, with a staff pointing to the celestial globe.  They were led by Apollo.

16. **Asclepios,** *Æsculapius,* god of healing, son of Apollo; represented as an old man, with a staff around which a serpent is twined; generally accompanied by Hygiēa *Health.* The chief seat of his worship was Epidaurus. — **Ilithyia,** *Lucīna,* goddess of birth.

17. The **Fates,** Μοῖραι, daughters of Night: Clotho, who spins the thread of life, with a spindle; Lachĕsis, who appoints man his fate, pointing to the horoscope on the globe, and Atrŏpos, the inexorable, with scales or scissors. — **Nemesis,** goddess of vengeance.

18. **Æolus,** god of the winds. — **Eos,** *Aurōra,* goddess of the morning, married to Tithōnus.

19. **Momus,** god of laughter. — **Morpheus,** god of sleep. — **Plutus,** god of riches. — **Hymen,** god of marriage.

## II. The Sea (Marine Gods).

20. **Poseidon,** *Neptune;* worshipped peculiarly at the Isthmic sanctuary, and at Tænărum: represented with wet locks, trident, and dolphin or horse. His wife is Amphitrīte (§ 22), and his chief companion Triton, blowing on a conch-shell. He was father to Polyphēmus, the man-eating Cyclops. — He contended with Athēna (§ 5) which should give the name to Athens; the honor was adjudged to Athēna for her creation of the olive-tree, which was decided to be a more valuable gift to man than that of the horse by Poseidon.

21. **Proteus,** a seer, living in the sea, and possessing the power of changing his form at will. — **Glaucus,** another sea-prophet, whose body ended in a fish's tail.

22. **Nereus,** (the calm sea,) with his daughters, the Nereids, or Sea-nymphs, the chief of whom are Amphitrīte and Thetis.

23. **Ino,** daughter of Cadmus (§ 38), and wife of Athămas (§ 45), being made mad by Hera, leapt into the sea with her son Melicertes; she became the goddess **Leucothea,** he the god **Palæmon.**

24. The **Sirens,** the "Muses of the Sea," treacherous and seductive, beguiling voyagers to their destruction. — **Scylla,** a monster with six dog's-heads, and twelve forelegs: the rest of her body concealed in a cave. Opposite is **Charybdis,** under a wild fig-tree; a fearful whirlpool. Supposed to have been at the Straits of Messina.

### III. The Earth (Chthonian Gods).

25. **Cybele** or **Rhea**, mother of the gods, accompanied by the Curētes; worshipped with peculiar rites by the Corybantes, in Phrygia (Mt. Ida, &c.); also worshipped in Crete.

26. **Dionysus** or **Bacchus**, son of Zeus and Semĕle; god of friendship, and wine; married to Ariadne on the island of Naxos. He was represented as crowned with ivy, sometimes young, sometimes bearded, carrying the *thyrsus*, a pole crowned with a pine-cone, or vine or ivy leaves. His expedition to India was celebrated. His Thiăsos, or company, consisted of Pan, the god of nature, with pointed ears and legs of a goat, playing on a pipe of reeds; Priāpus, the god of fertility; the Satyrs, sportive beings of merely animal nature, of human form with ears and tail of a goat; the Silēni, formed like the Satyrs, sometimes drunken, sometimes grave and noble; the Centaurs, horses with men's heads (the chief of whom was Chiron); the Nymphs, of whom the *Naiads* are of the water, the *Oreads* of the mountains, the *Dryads* of trees, (the *Hamadryads* attached to a single tree,) &c. — Among the Nymphs was Echo, who out of love for Narcissus faded away to a mere voice, while Narcissus died of love for his own reflection. — He was worshipped with wild nocturnal rites every other year at the winter solstice, by the women (Bacchæ or Mœnădes). Thebes was the chief seat of his worship in Greece, but it was peculiarly celebrated in Thrace and Asia Mi-

nor. — The origin of the Athenian Drama is connected with his festivals.

27. **Demeter**, *Ceres*, "Mother Earth," goddess of agriculture, and author, Θεσμοφόρος, of certain laws touching human life; worshipped with peculiar solemnity, together with her daughter Proserpine or Κόρη, and Dionȳsus, in the mysteries at Eleusis, once a year. Her symbols were a garland of ears of corn, and a poppy. She taught her art to Triptolĕmus, "the thrice-ploughing," who then instructed men in it.

28. The Cabīri of Lemnos and Samothrace practised strange rites, little understood, but perhaps similar to the Eleusinian Mysteries (§ 27).

### IV. The Lower Regions (Hades).

29. **Pluto**, or **Hades**, King of the Under-world; married **Persephone**, *Proserpine* (§ 27), daughter of Demēter, whom he stole from earth while gathering flowers: she spent half the year with him, half with her mother.

30. The rivers of Hades were the Styx, which formed the boundary, Achĕron, stream of woe, Pyriphlegĕthon, fire-stream, Cocȳtus, wailing-stream, and Lethe, oblivion. — Cerbĕrus, the three-headed dog, watched the entrance, and Charon ferried the souls of the dead, conducted to him by Hermes (§ 10), across the Styx.

31. The judges were Minos, Rhadamanthus, and Æăcus. They sent the souls of the good to Elysium, while the wicked were punished in Tartărus. The most

noted punishments were those of Tityus, whose liver was gnawed by two vultures; Tantălus (§ 41), placed in a pool the waters of which shrank from him when he wished to drink, and under a tree whose branches retreated when he would pluck the fruit; Sisўphus, a wicked K. of Corinth, forever rolling a stone up a hill; Ixīon (§ 50), bound hand and foot to a turning wheel; and the Danaīdæ (§ 39), bringing water in a sieve.

32. The Furies, 'Ερινύες, were Tisiphŏne, the deadly avenger, Alecto, the tireless pursuer, and Megæra, the terror-inspiring. They were also worshipped as Eumenides, the Well-wishing, Σεμναί, the August, and Πότνιαι, the Revered.

## V. Heroes and Demigods.

33. **Prometheus**, [tragedy by Æschўlus,] *forethought*, (son of Iapĕtus, §1,) outwitted Zeus in various ways. He stole fire from heaven, and gave it to men; according to some accounts he formed men. He was punished by being chained to a rock on Mt. Caucăsus, where an eagle fed upon his liver. His brother **Epimetheus**, *afterthought*, received from Zeus a beautiful woman, **Pandora**, *all-gifts*, to whom each of the gods had given some charm; she lifted the lid of the vessel in which all the ills of humanity were hidden, and let them escape, only hope remaining behind.

34. **Deucalion**, son of Prometheus, and his wife **Pyrrha**, the only persons saved from a deluge. Being told by an

oracle to throw their mother's bones behind them, they threw stones (the bones of their mother Earth), which were changed, those thrown by Deucalion into men, those by Pyrrha into women. He was father of Hellen, *eponyme* of the Greeks (i. e. who gave his name to the nation).

35. **Orpheus,** a musician of Thrace, whose music charmed the wild beasts and the forest-trees. When his wife Eurydice died, he won Pluto by the charms of his lyre to restore her to life, but lost her again by turning round to look upon her. He was torn in pieces by the Thracian women.

36. ARGOS. **Io** was loved by Zeus, and changed by him into a heifer, watched at Hera's command by the hundred-eyed Argos Panoptes. She was then driven by a gad-fly to Egypt. Her grandson **Danaus** returned to Argos, and when his fifty daughters the Danaïdæ (§ 31) married the fifty sons of his brother Ægyptus, they all except one slew their husbands at his command. — **Perseus** was descended from him, a son of Zeus and Danäe. With the aid of Athēna he killed the Gorgon Medūsa, a woman with snakes for hair, whose look turned the beholder into stone; the winged horse Pegāsus sprang from her blood. Perseus delivered Andromĕda from a dragon and married her.

37. **Heracles,** *Hercŭles,* [trag. by Euripĭdes,] was descended from Perseus (§ 36); son of Zeus and Alcmēne; he was condemned by Hera to perform twelve labors at the command of his cousin Eurystheus: — 1. To kill the Nemean lion: he always afterwards wore its hide.

2. To slay the Lernæan hydra, a monster with nine heads. 3. To subdue the Erymanthian boar. 4. To catch the brazen-footed hind of Arcadia, sacred to Artĕmis. 5. To destroy the Stymphalian birds. 6. To cleanse the stables of Augeas. 7. To capture the Cretan bull. 8. To bring to Mycēnæ the man-eating horses of K. Diomede of Thrace. 9. To get possession of the girdle of Hippolўte, Q. of the Amazons (§ 46). 10. To drive off the oxen of the giant Geryon. 11. To fetch the golden apples from the gardens of the Hesperĭdes (daughters of the heaven-supporting Atlas). 12. To bring Cerbĕrus (§ 30) from the Infernal Regions (he descended by the entrance at Tænărum).— He was killed by a poisoned tunic given him by his wife in a fit of jealousy.

38. THEBES. Cadmus came from Phœnicia in search of his sister Eurōpa, who had been carried off by Zeus, in the shape of a white bull. At Thebes he killed a dragon and sowed its teeth in the earth, from which sprang armed men, who all slew each other except five, who were the ancestors of the Thebans.— Œdipus, [tragedies by Sophocles,] one of his descendants, was son of Laïus and Jocasta; he killed Laius in ignorance, and married Jocasta, after solving the enigma of the Sphinx (a monster with the body of a lion and the head of a woman); thus becoming K. of Thebes. His sons, Eteocles and Polynīces, quarrelled, which occasioned the war of the "Seven against Thebes" [trag. by Æschylus]. The two brothers killed each other; their sister Antigŏne [trag. by Sophocles] buried the body of Polynīces in defiance of the edict of the tyrant Creon.

39. ATHENS. **Cecrops** and **Erichthonius** or **Erechtheus** were autochthons (i. e. sprung from the earth), and kings of Athens; Erechtheus had in part the form of a serpent. — Philomēla and Procne were daughters of Pandīon, son of Erichthonius. Procne was married to Tereus, K. of the Thracians, who dishonored Philomēla and tore out her tongue. She was changed into a nightingale, Procne into a swallow, and Tereus into a hoopoe. — **Theseus,** son of K. Ægeus, was the national hero of Athens. He killed the Minotaur (half man, half bull) in the Labyrinth of K. Minos in Crete, fought with the Amazons (§ 46), and founded many excellent institutions in Athens. Forgetting on his return from Crete to hoist white sails as signal of his safety, his father in despair threw himself into the sea, hence called *Æge'an.* — His son Hippolȳtus unjustly incurred his displeasure and was cursed by him; upon which Poseidon frightened the horses of Hippolȳtus, who dragged him till he was dead.

40. SPARTA. The **Dioscuri,** Διὸς κοῦροι, were sons of Leda; **Castor** (and his sister Clytæmnestra, wife of Agamemnon, § 41), by Tyndareus; **Polydeuces,** *Pollux*, (and his sister Helen, wife of Menelāus, § 41,) by Zeus. Polydeuces was therefore immortal, but shared his immortality with his brother; he was noted for boxing, Castor for horsemanship.

41. FAMILY OF TANTĂLUS, upon which a special curse rested. **Tantalus** (§ 31), a king in Asia Minor, was a favorite of the gods, to whom, to test them, he served up the flesh of his own son **Pelops.** Pelops, restored to life,

went to Greece, and gave his name to the Peloponnēsus.—
His sons, **Atreus** and **Thyestes**, quarrelled, and Atreus
served up the sons of Thyestes (*Thyeste'an banquet*) to
their father. The sons of Atreus were **Agamemnon**, K. of
Mycēnæ, and **Menelaus**, K. of Sparta (§§ 42 ff).— **Niobe**,
daughter of Tantălus, boasted of her twelve children above
those of Leto (§ 6); at the request of their mother, Apollo
and Artĕmis slew them all; Niŏbe was then changed into
stone.

42. When **Peleus** and Thetis (§ 22) were married, all
the gods were invited except **Eris**, *Discord*, who in revenge threw among the guests a golden apple inscribed
"To the most beautiful." Hera, Athēna, and Aphrodīte
contended for it, and chose **Paris**, or **Alexander**,—son of
**Priam**, K. of Troy, and **Hecŭba** [trag. by Euripĭdes],—
to decide between them; Hera promising him sovereignty
and wealth, Athēna glory, Aphrodīte the hand of Helen
(§ 40), the fairest woman in the world. He decided in
favor of Aphrodīte, abandoned his wife Œnōne, and stole
Helen from her husband.

43. TROJAN WAR. The Greek chiefs went under the
lead of Agamemnon (§ 41) to reclaim Helen (§ 42).
Being detained at Aulis, **Iphigenia** [tragedies of Euripi-
des], daughter of Agamemnon, was sacrificed to appease
Artĕmis. After a siege of ten years, Troy was taken by
means of a wooden horse, and sacked.— The most renowned of the Greek leaders were **Nestor** of Pylus, famed
for his wisdom; **Ulysses** of Ithăca, son of Laërtes, for
his cunning; **Achilles**, son of Peleus and Thetis (§ 42),

the bravest of the Greeks, K. of the Myrmidons (a people sprung from ants) in Thessaly; **Ajax** [trag. by Sophocles], son of **Telamon**, of Salamis, and **Diomedes**, son of Tydeus, of Argos, the two ranking next to Achilles; **Ajax** the Less, son of Oïleus, of Locris; **Idomeneus**, K. of Crete; and **Philoctetes** [trag. by Sophocles], the best archer in the army. The soothsayer was **Calchas**. — The chiefs of the Trojans were **Hector** and **Deiphobus**, sons of Priam, Æneas, son of Anchises and Aphrodīte, **Sarpedon**, and **Antenor**. Andromăche [trag. by Euripides] was wife of Hector, and Astyănax his son. Cassandra, daughter of Priam, was a prophetess condemned by Apollo never to be believed. — Hector was killed by Achilles in revenge for his friend Patroclus. Achilles was killed with an arrow by Paris, and Ajax slew himself in a fit of madness, because the armor of Achilles was adjudged to Ulysses rather than himself. The Lesser Ajax was dashed on a rock by Athēna. Homer's Iliad relates some of the events of the siege.

44. After the capture of Troy (§ 43), Ænēas went to Italy, on his way visiting Queen Dido in Carthage; his adventures are narrated in Virgil's Ænēid. His son **Ascanius**, or **Iulus**, was ancestor of the kings of Alba, and, as was supposed, of the Julian *gens* (§ 127). — Homer's Odyssey contains the wanderings of Ulysses for ten years, during which he met with the Cyclops Polyphēmus (§ 20), the Sirens (§ 24), the sorceress Circe, and the nymph Calypso. His wife Penelŏpe was beset with suitors in his absence, whom she put off under pre-

tence of finishing a piece of cloth in her loom, while she unravelled every night what she had done in the day. His son Telemăchus went in search of his father under guidance of Athēna, in the form of Mentor. When Ulysses reached home he was recognized only by his nurse and old dog Argus.—On Agamemnon's return to Mycēnæ he was murdered [trag. by Æschy̆lus] by his wife Clytæmnestra (§ 40) and her paramour Ægisthus. His son **Orestes** [trag. by Euripides] avenged him by killing both, for which deed he was pursued by the Eumenides (§ 32), [trag. by Æschylus,] and consoled by his sister Electra [tragedies by Sophocles and Euripides].

45. ARGONAUTIC EXPEDITION. The ram with the Golden Fleece had swum from Thessaly to Colchis, carrying Phrixos and Helle, children of Athămas; but Helle being drowned gave her name to the Hellespont. **Jason** went in the ship Argo to recover the Fleece. On the way his companions drove the Harpies, filthy and ravenous birds, from the table of K. Phineus. **Medea** [trag. by Euripides], a famous sorceress, helped Jason obtain the fleece, and married him.

46. **Amazons**, a warlike race of women, upon the R. Thermōdon. They invaded Greece under their Q. Hippoly̆te, who was defeated and married by Theseus (§ 39). They also brought aid to the Trojans (§ 43).

47. **Meleager** killed the Calydonian boar. His mother, Althæa, kept a brand plucked from the fire, on which his life depended; when he killed her brothers in a quarrel, she threw the brand in the fire.

48. **Bellerophon** killed the Chimæra, a monster with the head of a lion, the body of a goat, and the tail of a dragon.

49. **Admetus**, a king of Thessaly, whose flocks Apollo tended. When he was about to die, his life was promised on condition that any one would die for him, and these terms were accepted by his wife Alcestis [trag. by Euripides].

50. **Lapithæ**, a rude people of Thessaly, who fought with the Centaurs (§ 26); among them were Ixīon (§ 31), noted for his treachery, and his son Pirithŏus, who descended to Hades with Theseus (§ 39) to rescue Proserpine.

51. **Amphion and Zethus**, sons of Zeus and Antiŏpe; Zethus fierce, Amphīon gentle, skilled on the lyre, by the aid of which he built the walls of Thebes. They bound Dirce, who had plotted against their mother's life, to a wild bull, which they turned loose.

52. **Atalanta**, famed for swiftness of foot. Her hand was promised to whoever would outstrip her, which Milanion accomplished by dropping golden apples in her path.

53. **Dædalus**, built the Cretan Labyrinth (§ 39); imprisoned by K. Minos, he made wings fastened with wax, for himself and his son Icărus, who flew so high, however, that the sun melted the wax, and he fell into the sea, which was called from him *Icarian*.

54. **Marsyas**, a satyr of Phrygia, who vied on his flute with Apollo's lyre; being vanquished, he was flayed alive by Apollo.

# ROMAN MYTHOLOGY.

55. **Janus,** the god of *opening;* the first day of every month was sacred to him; represented with a double face, generally bearded. His temple was open in time of war, and shut in time of peace.

56. **Jupiter;** the root is the same as *Zeus* (§ 2) with *pater* added. Jupiter S t a t o r was the guardian of Rome; to Jupiter F e r e t r i u s were offered the *spolia opīma,* when the commander of the enemy was slain by the Roman general.

57. **Mars,** the patron deity of Rome, held in high honor throughout Italy; Mars G r a d ī v u s, father of Romŭlus, was the god of the Salii (§ 149). It was a Sabine custom to consecrate to Mars all male children born in a certain spring (called *ver sacrum*), who when they were grown up went off by themselves and formed a settlement. This was the origin of the Samnites and the Lucanians. — **Bellona,** goddess of war.

58. **Quirinus,** the Sabine Mars, special divinity of Cures (same root as *Cures, Quirītes, Quirinālis,* &c.). In later times identified with Romŭlus.

59. **Juno,** the feminine form of *Jupiter;* as **Lucina** she was goddess of birth.

60. **Minerva,** goddess of wisdom, and of handicrafts. — In the Capitolium, or Temple of Jupiter upon the Capitoline, Minerva had a cell at the right, Juno at the left of that of Jupiter, according to Etruscan usage.

61. **Diana,** the feminine form of Janus (*Dianus*); goddess of the moon; she had a noted sanctuary, *Nemus*, near Aricia (Lake *Nemi*).

62. **Neptune,** god of the sea. — **Consus,** at whose festival, *Consualia* (§ 173), the Sabine women were carried off, is sometimes identified with Neptune.

63. **Vulcan,** or **Mulciber,** god of fire and of the smithy.

64. **Liber Pater,** god of freedom and joy; identified with Bacchus; at his festival, *Liberalia* (§ 173), young men assumed the *toga virīlis* (§ 180).

65. **Ceres,** goddess of the earth; there were festivals of Ceres, Liber, and *Libĕra,* in imitation of the Greek worship of Demētēr, Dionȳsus, and Cora (§ 27).

66. **Mercury,** god of traffic; **Terminus,** of boundaries.

67. **Venus,** goddess of love and beauty; Venus Genetrix was especially honored by the Julian gens as their ancestor (see §§ 43 and 44).

68. **Vesta,** goddess of the hearth. She was served by six Virgins of noble birth, whose parents must both be living (*patrĭma et matrĭma*). It was their duty to keep the eternal fire burning upon her altar; they were vowed to virginity, and if found guilty of breaking the vow were buried alive.

69. The **Penates,** or household gods, and the **Genius,** both of the family and the individual, were worshipped with

great honor. The Penātes were brought by Ænēas (§ 44) to Lavinium, where they were especially reverenced.

70. **Saturn** and **Ops**, the old Italian god and goddess of the Earth: he was represented with a sickle. From him Italy was sometimes called Saturnia.

71. **Vejovis**, the "evil Jove," a harmful divinity. — **Diespiter** was the name of Jupiter as god of the Fetiales (§ 150) and guardians of faith.

72. **Mater Matuta**, goddess of birth, also of harbors. — **Bona Dea** or **Maia**, goddess of increase; worshipped by women alone on the first of May (§ 173). — **Aurora**, goddess of the morning.

73. **Apollo Soranus**, worshipped on Mt. Soracte; certain families were consecrated to his service and called *Hirpi* (wolves). — **Semo Sancus**, or **Dius Fidius**, *god of faith*, a Sabine god, whose name was used in oaths.

74. **Pales**, goddess of herds, worshipped in the festival *Palilia* (§ 173), the anniversary of the founding of Rome. Other rural deities were **Picus**, **Faunus** and **Fauna** (cf. Pan and Satyrs, § 26; the feast *Lupercalia*, § 173, was in honor of Faunus, celebrated by the Luperci, clad in goatskins), **Silvanus** (of woods), **Feronia** (who had a grove near Mt. Soracte, where fairs were held), **Flora** (of flowers), **Vertumnus** (of fruits), and **Pomona** (of the orchard).

75. **Orcus**, god of death; **Dis Pater**, god of the Underworld. — The spirits of the dead were called **Manes**. The **Lares** were the glorified spirits of the good, especially of ancestors; the *lar familiāris* of a house was its founder and protector. The **Larvæ** and **Lemures** were evil spirits,

wandering about by night. — The **Parcæ**, Nona, Decŭma, and Morta, presiding over birth; afterwards identified with the Greek Fates (§ 17).

76. **Dii Indigetes**, deified heroes; as Æneas (§ 44).

77. Temples were erected by the Romans to many *abstract qualities;* e. g. **Pavor** and **Pallor, Honos** and **Virtus, Concordia, Libertas, Pudicitia,** and above all **Fors Fortuna** (worshipped especially at Præneste and Antium).

78. **Juno Sospita** Mater Regīna, one of the most widely reverenced deities of Latium: represented with shield, spear, goat-skin helmet and mantle, and pointed shoes; her chief sanctuary was at Lanuvium, where she had a flamen (§ 148).

*∗* The worship of the following divinities was introduced from Greece.

79. **Apollo** (§ 6); introduced very early, and becoming very wide-spread. The Sibyls were his prophetesses, the chief of whom in Italy were the Cumæan and the Tiburtine (there was a temple of the Sibyl at Tibur).

80. **Cybele,** or **Idæa Mater** (§ 25), introduced B. C. 207, at the direction of the Sibylline books (§ 145); received by P. Scipio Nasīca, as being "optimus Romanorum."

81. **Æsculapius** (§ 6); introduced B. C. 291, after a pestilence, by the same authority. The holy serpent was brought from Epidaurus, and, when the ship arrived in the Tiber, crept upon the island, which was afterwards sacred to Æsculapius.

82. The worship of **Hercules** (§ 37), and that of **Castor**

and **Pollux** (§ 40), were introduced early, and became prominent in Roman mythology. Hercules killed the robber Cacus; Castor and Pollux aided the Romans in the battle of Lake Regillus. The worship of Hercules belonged to the two gentes Potitii and Pinarii, the latter being inferior because they arrived late when the rites were established. Afterwards the Potitii sold the knowledge of the rites, which were thenceforward conducted by public slaves; the Potitii all perished in consequence of this act of impiety.

83. **Bacchus** (§ 26); the secret and indecent rites of Bacchus began to get a foothold among the citizens, but were suppressed B. C. 186.

84. Under the empire many Oriental observances were introduced, particularly, from Egypt, the worship of **Isis** (§ 86), represented with a lotos-flower and a knot tied upon her breast; and **Serapis**, of sombre countenance, the head surrounded with sun's rays, and with the *modius* for a cap; also from Persia that of **Mithras**, a god of light, whose worship was symbolized by the figure of a man slaying a bull, whose blood is tasted by a dog, a serpent, and a scorpion.

# EGYPTIAN MYTHOLOGY.

85. **Ammon,** *Jupiter,* the great god of Thebes, represented with a ram's head or horns. He had a famous oracle in Libya.

86. **Osiris,** *Bacchus,* and **Isis,** *Ceres,* his sister and wife. A great benefactor, who taught the cultivation of the earth. He was killed by his brother **Set,** *Typhon,* but his soul was supposed to live in the holy bull **Apis,** at Memphis, while he himself ruled over the lower world as **Serapis.**

87. **Horus,** *Apollo* (*Horapollo*), son of Osiris and Isis; known also as **Harpocrates,** god of silence, born with his finger on his lips, and so represented. — **Anubis,** son of Osiris (with a dog's head), was the companion of Isis, and the conductor of souls to the Under-world.

88. **Phthah,** *Vulcan,* chief god of Memphis; **Neith,** *Minerva,* chief deity of Saïs; **Pacht,** or **Bubastis,** *Diana,* represented with a cat's head; **Seb,** *Saturn,* whose symbol was the goose; **Thoth,** *Mercury,* to whom the ibis was sacred; **Savak,** the crocodile-god; **Athor,** *Venus;* **Nepthys,** *Vesta.*

# ANTIQUITIES.

# GRECIAN ANTIQUITIES.

## I. ATHENS.

89. THE government of Athens, originally a monarchy, became afterwards an oligarchy. Its early institutions were attributed to Theseus (§ 39), who made Athens capital of Attica, and established the **Prytaneum**, or national hearth, where a perpetual fire was kept burning. As in all Ionic cities, the citizens were divided according to birth into 4 **Tribes,** φῦλον or φυλή, each subdivided into 3 **Phratriæ,** φρατρία (cf. Curia, § 123), and each phratria into 30 **Gentes,** γένος (cf. Gens, § 127). This division continued even after the reforms of Clisthĕnes (§ 92), as a means of preserving the purity and legitimacy of descent.

90. Side by side with this division was another into 12 **Trittyes,** τριττύς, (3 to each tribe,) and 48 **Naucraries,** ναυκραρία. The nobles were called *Eupatrids,* Εὐπατρίδαι; the people as a political body were called Δῆμος.

91. This aristocratic constitution was changed by Solon, B. C. 594, into one based upon wealth, Timocracy; the citizens being divided according to landed property into four **Classes,** of which only the first enjoyed full political rights,

the fourth, the **Thetes,** being excluded from all offices, as well as free from taxes and regular military service.

92. Clisthĕnes, B. C. 510, founded the Democracy, admitting all free inhabitants, without distinction of birth or wealth, to a share in the government; and his reforms were still further carried out by Aristīdes and Pericles. Clisthĕnes created ten new tribes in place of the old four, among which he distributed the **Demes,** δῆμοι (towns and villages), of Attica, without regard to juxtaposition. — An individual was designated by giving his own name, that of his father, and that of the deme; e. g. Demosthĕnes, son of Demosthĕnes, a Pæanian (Δημοσθένης Δημοσθένους Παιανιεύς).

93. Besides the citizens, there were always in Athens a large number of resident foreigners (**Metics,** μέτοικοι), and about three quarters of all the inhabitants of Attica were slaves. — The whole population in the time of Demosthĕnes appears to have been about 500,000, of whom about 20,000 were citizens.

## 94. Archons.

Established on the expulsion of the kings, and inheriting their power; at first one, afterwards nine in number, chosen annually, and after the time of Clisthĕnes (§ 92) by lot. In historical time their functions were chiefly judicial, e. g. presiding in the Heliastic courts (§ 97). They were: — 1. The **Archon Eponymus,** from whom the year was named, whose jurisdiction was in cases involving the interests of families; e. g. inheritance, the property of widows and orphans, etc. 2. The **King Archon,** who presided at certain festivals, and in trials where the religion of the state was involved, including sacrilege and murder. 3. The Polemarch, originally commander-in-chief, afterwards having jurisdiction over foreigners and *metics* (§ 93). (Cf. Prætor Peregrīnus, § 131.) 4. The six Thesmothetæ, whose jurisdiction extended to all cases not specially provided for.

### 95. Ephetæ.

A court of 51 judges, established by Draco, B. C. 624. They were presided over by the King Archon (§ 94), and tried cases of homicide, sitting in five different places according to the circumstances of the homicide. After Solon gave jurisdiction in cases of wilful murder to the Senate of Areopăgus (§ 96), they sat in only four places; in later times they lost all importance, and sank to a mere form.

96. Senate of Areopagus. Ἡ ἐν Ἀρείῳ πάγῳ Βουλή.

The Court of Areopagus was established, or at least remodelled, by Solon, to try cases of wilful murder, etc., which had before probably belonged to the Ephĕtæ (§ 95). It was composed of ex-archons (§ 94), who, on completing their term of office without disgrace, became members for life. Before the time of Pericles, and after the Peloponnesian War, it exercised also a censorial power (cf. Censors, § 132) over the private life and religious customs of the Athenians, and was always regarded by them with peculiar reverence, its influence being felt as a check upon the democratical tendencies of the state.

## 97. Dicasteries.

Each year the archons drew by lot the names of 6,000 citizens, of over thirty years, 600 from each tribe; which body, called the **Heliæa,** was divided into 10 sections of 500 each, called **Dicasteries,** 1,000 being kept in reserve to supply vacancies (one of these being also added to each dicastery in order to make an odd number). In important cases, two, three, or even more dicasteries often sat together as a single court. Almost all judicial questions, except those belonging to the Areopăgus (§ 96), came in the course of time to be intrusted to these dicasteries. Each *dicast* received three obols (§ 197) a day.

## Senate of Five Hundred. Ἡ Βουλή.

98. Established by Solon, consisting of 400 members, 100 from each tribe (§ 89). By Clisthĕnes the number was increased to 500, 50 being taken by lot from each of the new tribes (§ 92). This constituted a natural division into ten sections, the members of which, all belonging to the same tribe, were called **Prytanes,** πρυτάνεις. Each section in turn had (by lot) the presidency in the Senate (hence it was called the *prytanizing tribe*) for one tenth of a year, called a *prytany;* and every day the Prytanes chose an **Epistates** from their own number to preside in the Senate or the Assembly (§ 100), and keep the keys of the treasury and archives. It was the duty of the Prytanes to meet every day (except festival days) during their prytany, but the Senators from the other tribes might be absent. In later

times the Epistates selected one member from each of the non-prytanizing tribes, nine in all, called **Proedri**, to represent these tribes in the Senate ; and from these Proedri a second Epistates was chosen as their representative, to preside in both Senate and Assembly.

99. The primary office of the Senate was to prepare matter for the action of the Assembly, in the form of προβουλεύματα, or preliminary bills. When any such was charged with being illegal, the person making it was indicted by γραφὴ παρανόμων. — The Senate was the chief executive power in the state, had the regulation of finance, and decided on the qualifications of magistrates. Each member received a drachma (§ 197) a day.

100. ASSEMBLY. Ἐκκλησία.

Four regular meetings of the Assembly were held during each prytany (§ 98), — either in the Agora, the Pnyx, or later the Dionysiac Theatre, — and extraordinary ones at other times. It was the duty of every citizen twenty years old to attend. All subjects of general interest — public expenditures, taxes, alliances, appointment of state officers, matters of religion, etc. — legitimately came before the Assembly, the vote after discussion being taken generally by hand. It also exercised certain judicial functions, but its legislative power was limited, as it could only pass temporary decrees, ψηφίσματα, upon matters presented to it by the Senate (§ 99). — To the people in their assembly belonged the right of banishing an obnoxious or dangerous citizen for ten, afterwards five years, by **Ostracism**, in which

4 *

they voted with oyster-shells or potsherds inscribed with the name of the person to be banished; 6,000 votes were necessary to condemn. — Three obols (§ 197) a day were received by every person attending the Assembly.

### 101. Νομοθεται, &c.

At the first public assembly of each year it was lawful to propose any changes in existing laws, which were then left to a judicial committee, νομοθέται, taken from the Heliæa (§ 97), and probably presided over by the Thesmothĕtæ (§ 94). The question was argued before them as before a court, and they had full power to preserve or repeal. — The Νομοφύλακες were persons intrusted by Pericles with the power, which had previously belonged to the Areopăgus, of testing the legality of amendments to the προβουλεύματα before they were brought before the Assembly.

### 102. Later Changes.

During the Peloponnesian War, B. C. 411, an aristocratical reaction placed the power in the hands of a committee of *Four Hundred*, while an assembly of five thousand wealthy citizens, which, however, never was called together, was to take the place of the Assembly. After four months the Democracy was restored. — After the power of Athens was crippled by the battle of Ægospotămi, B. C. 405, the Spartans gave the government to a committee of Thirty, who were overthrown by Thrasybūlus, B. C. 403.

## 103. Liturgies.

These were personal services rendered to the state by the wealthy citizens. The most important of the ordinary ones were the **Choregia,** or duty of providing the chorus for festivals and dramatic exhibitions, and the **Gymnasiarchia,** or duty of bearing the expenses of gymnastic exhibitions. — The **Trierarchy** was an extraordinary one, and consisted in the duty of fitting out and commanding a public ship. The original method was for a single wealthy individual to undertake this charge ; but a new system was adopted early in the 4th cent. B. C., by which 1,200 of the richest citizens were divided into 20 **Symmories,** and each of these into four companies, συντέλειαι, each of which companies of fifteen men supported one ship, and provided a commander. This plan was superseded by that of Demosthĕnes, which imposed the expense of a single ship upon every ten talents (§ 197) of taxable property.

## 104. Finances.

The Senate (§ 95) had the control of the revenues, but the direct management was in the hands of a Superintendent, chosen by the people for a term of four years ; this office was held by Aristīdes. The revenue consisted in rents, duties, tribute from subject states, fines, liturgies (§ 103), and on extraordinary occasions in a direct tax, εἰσφορά. For this purpose the people were divided into symmories resembling those of the trierarchies (§ 103).

*⁎* For Military Affairs, see § 119.

## II. SPARTA.

105. The Lacedæmonians were divided into two classes; the **Spartans,** or Doric conquerors, and the **Periœci,** Περίοικοι, who were free, but without the full rights of citizenship. Later, a distinction arose among the Spartans, as some were unable from poverty to furnish their proportion to the Syssitia or public tables. Those who fulfilled these requirements, and were brought up according to the prescribed forms, were termed Ὅμοιοι (*peers*). The slaves were called **Helots.**

### 106. Kings.

There were two kings, descended from the two *Heraclid* (see Chronology, B. C. 1104) brothers, **Procles** and **Eurysthenes.** They had little power beyond presiding in the Council, and commanding in war.

### 107. Ephors.

Five in number, entering upon their office at the autumnal equinox; the method of their election is unknown. They had very extensive judicial power, even over the kings, and gradually acquired the supreme executive power, two of them generally accompanying the king on his campaigns. The first of the five gave his name to the year.

### 108. Council, Γερουσία.

Established by Lycurgus, consisting of 28 men, none of whom could be under 60. It took the initiative in all legislation, and exercised judicial functions.

## 109. Assembly. Ἐκκλησία.

Every citizen of 30 years could take part. It had the power to vote (but without discussion) upon propositions of the kings or council; this vote was taken by acclamation.

## 110. Education.

Every child was taken from his parents and educated by the state, the only aim being to make vigorous and skilful soldiers. Reading and writing were confined to what was absolutely indispensable, but music was much cultivated within certain traditional limits.

*⁎* For Military Affairs, see § 120.

---

### III. AMPHICTYONIC COUNCIL.

111. An assembly originating in pre-historic times, and composed of deputies from 12 tribes; each tribe, whatever the number or size of the cities which represented it, having two members. Thus Sparta, a Doric state, had no more power to cast the Dorian vote than Doris or Cnidus. Meetings were held in the spring at Delphi, in the temple of Apollo; in the autumn, at Thermopylæ, in the temple of Demētēr. Originally it was a sort of religious partnership, and was valuable as a bond of union between the tribes. Its most important functions were to act as

guardians of the Delphian temple, and preside over the Pythian Games (§ 113); but it usurped at various times authority over the political and social interests of the states, and its influence was felt throughout Greece to a late period, often seriously for evil.

## IV. GAMES AND FESTIVALS.

### NATIONAL.

**112. Olympic Games.** — At Olympia, in honor of Zeus. They were held once in four years (πενταετηρίς), at the first full moon after the summer solstice (Attic month Hecatombæon, § 203), continuing five days. The prize was a crown of wild olive. The contests consisted of foot, horse, and chariot races, wrestling, boxing, etc. The Pentathlon — consisting of leaping (ἅλμα), running (δρόμος), throwing the quoit (δίσκος) and spear (ἀκόντιον), and wrestling (πάλη) — was a principal feature.

**113. Pythian Games.** — At Delphi, in honor of Apollo; held in the latter part of the summer, in the third year of every Olympiad. The prize was a laurel chaplet. Musical and artistic contests were especially encouraged in these games.

**114. Nemean Games.** — At Nemea, in honor of Zeus; in the spring of the first and the summer of the fourth year of each Olympiad. The prize was a wreath of olive, afterwards of parsley.

115. **Isthmian Games.** — Near Corinth, in honor of Poseidon; in the middle of summer, in the first and third year of each Olympiad. The prize was a chaplet of ivy, later of pine.

### Local.

#### 116. *Athenian.*

*Month* (§ 203).

Hecat. — **Panathenæa.** — To Athēna; 25th to 28th days, the third year of every Olympiad.

The *Lesser Panathenæa* came yearly.

Boedr. — **Eleusinia.** — Mysteries of Demēter (§ 27), in Eleusis; continuing twelve days.

Pyan. — **Theseia.** — Festival of Theseus (§ 39); 8th day.

**Thesmophoria.** — To Demēter; 11th to 13th.

**Apaturia.** — Of most of the Ionians. Festival of φράτριαι (§ 89), etc.

Poseid. — **Dionysia** (§ 28) μικρά or κατ' ἀγρούς. (Origin of Comedy.)

Gam. — **Lenæa.** — 11th to 13th. — Second festival of Dionȳsus.

Anth. — **Anthesteria.** — 11th to 13th. — Third of the Dionysiac festivals.

Elaph. — **Dionysia** μεγάλα or ἐν ἄστει. — 9th to 15th. (Origin of Tragedy.)

#### 117. *Other Parts of Greece.*

Attica. — **Brauronia.** — At Brauron, to Artĕmis (§ 7), once in four years.

| | |
|---|---|
| Thebes. | — **Daphnephoria.** — In honor of Apollo, every ninth year. |
| Plataea. | — **Eleutheria.** — Commemorative of the victory; once in four years. |
| Argos. | — **Heraea** or **Hecatombaea.** — To Hera (§ 3); once in four years, with games. |
| Epidaurus. | — **Asclepiea.** — To Asclepios (§ 16), once in four years. |
| Arcadia. | — **Lycaea.** — On M. Lycæus, in honor of Zeus (§ 2); very ancient. |
| Laconia. | — **Hyacinthia.** — At Amÿclæ, to Apollo (§ 6); at midsummer, for three days. |
| Delos. | — **Delia.** — Every four years, in honor of Apollo and Artĕmis. |
| Ionia. | — **Panionia.** — At Mt. Mycăle, to Poseidon (§ 20). |

## V. COLONIES.

118. THESE were of two kinds: — 1. 'Αποικίαι, which were entirely independent of the mother city, μητρόπολις. 2. Κληρουχίαι, in which the colonists still remained citizens of the *metropolis* (cf. Roman Colonies, § 151). The former took with them sacred fire from the *Prytanēum* (§ 89) of the *metropolis*, the latter considered the original fire in the Prytanēum as still their own.

## VI. MILITARY.

119. The characteristic feature of the Grecian military was the Phalanx, or compact body of soldiers. Of the Athenian army we only know that the heavy-armed soldiers, ὁπλῖται, were divided into τάξεις and λόχοι, the cavalry into ἴλαι. Ten generals, στρατηγοί, were chosen annually to command the army; under them were ten ταξίαρχοι for the foot, and two ἵππαρχοι for the cavalry. By the reforms of Iphicrates, shortly after the Peloponnesian War, the light-armed troops, πελτασταί, acquired greater importance.

120. The Spartan army, comprising all the citizens between 20 and 60, was divided into six μόραι, each commanded by a Polemarch. To each μόρα there were 4 λόχοι, 8 πεντηκοστύες, and 16 ἐνωμοτίαι. Each of these divisions contained cavalry as well as infantry; their strength when in actual service seems to have varied. There were also 300 *knights*, ἱππεῖς, forming a body-guard for the king.

121. The Macedonian phalanx was distinguished by its immobility. Very long spears were used, those of the fifth rank projecting three feet in front of the first rank.

# ROMAN ANTIQUITIES.

## I. DIVISIONS OF THE PEOPLE.

122. The **Patricians** were citizens in full righ'; the **Plebeians** were inferior, and, to a certain extent, subject, until equality was established by the Licinian Laws. B. C. 367. The Roman people in their civil capacity were called *Quirītes*. The body of citizens, originally the Paricians alone, were called *Popŭlus* (cf. Δῆμος, § 90).

123. The Patricians were originally divided into three tribes,— the **Ramnes** (Latin), **Tities** (Sabine), and **Luceres** (perhaps Etruscan),— but these divisions were of no historical importance. Each tribe was divided into ten **Curiæ**, at the head of each of which was a **Curio**.

124. The city was also divided into four local tribes, **Suburana, Esquilina, Collina,** and **Palatina**. As the territory was extended, thirty-one country tribes were added. The city tribes were the least respectable.

125. For military purposes, the citizens were divided by King Servius Tullius into five **Classes** (cf. § 91), according to wealth, and these into 193 **Centuries**, the whole people thus forming the army (cf. § 129). The census of the first

class was 100,000 *asses* (§ 198), and of the others, 75,000, 50,000, 25,000, and 11,000 *asses*. The first class contained 80 centuries, the fifth 30, the others 20 each; half of these centuries consisted of *seniores* (over 45 years of age), the rest of *juniores*. There were also 18 centuries of Equites *equo publico* (having a horse assigned by the state), who had the census of the first class; four centuries of workmen; and one of poor citizens, *capite censi*.

126. After the equalization of the Patricians and Plebeians, a new aristocracy grew up, of the *Nobĭles*. The *Novi homines*, of whom were Marius and Cicero, were those none of whose ancestors had held curule office (§ 129). — The *Optimātes* and *Populāres* were the members of the conservative and radical parties. — The Equestrian Order, *Ordo Equestris*, was an aristocracy of wealth, brought into existence by the legislation of C. Gracchus (§ 171), B. C. 121, and generally hostile to the Senate.

127. The people were also divided into **Gentes**, the members of which claimed a common origin, and had common *sacra*, or sacred rites. The *nomen* of every man was that of his *gens*, which always ended in *ius* (except a few Etruscan names in *na*); the *prænōmen* was the individual name, the *cognōmen* that of the family; the *agnōmen* was a personal name acquired by some exploit; e. g. *Publius Cornelius Scipio Africānus*. Women were called simply by the name of the gens, as *Cornelia;* the daughters being distinguished as *prima, secunda*, &c.

128. There was also a peculiar personal relation between a patrician or nobleman as **Patron**, and his **Clients**.

The patron was the legal representative and the defender of his clients, who in turn owed him aid and service. — Manumitted slaves were called **Liberti** in relation to their former master, or **Libertini** as a class; they continued to owe service to their former master as patron. Legally, slaves could hold no property, but they were permitted by usage to keep a part of their earnings, called Peculium.

## II. MAGISTRATES.

129. AFTER the expulsion of the kings, B. C. 509, Rome was a Republic. The magistrates were chosen annually, with the exception of the Censors and Dictators. They are divided into **Greater** and **Lesser**, according as they possessed the greater or lesser *auspices* (§ 146). — The **Curule** Magistrates had the right to use the *Sella curūlis*, or curule chair of ivory; all of these were Greater Magistrates (*Majores*), except the Curule Ædiles (§ 134). — All of these magistrates were absolute, each in his sphere, during their term of office, but liable to be called to account at its close. They received a religious consecration, and could not legally be deposed. The same person might hold civil, military, naval, judicial, and religious offices. The word *facere* was used of the people, *creare* of the magistrate who presided at the comitia when the choice was made.

## 1. Greater Magistrates.

130. **Consuls.** Two in number, having the chief executive power. They went into office, in the 3d cent. B. C., on the Ides of March, but after B. C. 153 (inclusive), on the Kalends of January. 43 was the legal age for holding the office. Each Consul was preceded in public by 12 **Lictors** with axes in bundles of rods (*fasces*). If the term of office of the Consuls expired before their successors were elected, the Patrician part of the Senate chose an **Interrex**, whose office lasted only five days, when he created a second, whose duty it was to hold the election. Sometimes several *interrēges* succeeded before a Consul could be chosen. After the term of office of the Consul expired, he was often sent as **Proconsul** to govern a Province; and by Sulla (B. C. 82) it was made the law that the Consuls should be so sent, while during their year of office they should remain in Italy.

131. **Prætors.** At first one, afterwards two, then six in number, increased by Sulla to eight; they must be 40 years of age. They exercised judicial powers; the Prætor **Urbanus** between citizens, the **Peregrinus** (cf. *Archon Polemarch*, § 94) for foreigners; the others originally held command in the Provinces, but afterwards presided over special courts, *Quæstiōnes* (§ 171). They were sent as **Proprætors** to rule the Provinces after their term of office expired.

132. **Censors.** Two in number, chosen once in five years, for a term of eighteen months. They held a census of the people in the Campus Martius, decided upon their citizenship, made out the list of the members of the Senate, and

had a general supervision of the morals of the state, with power to inflict disgraceful punishments (see § 161). They also farmed out the public revenues (§ 172), and conducted the most important public works, such as the building of aqueducts and military roads.

133. **Dictator.** Appointed in time of need for a term of six months, and possessing kingly powers in full: the **Magister Equitum** was his second in command. He was accompanied by twenty-four Lictors. After the second Punic war the office disappeared, its place being taken by the dictatorial powers conferred by the Senate upon the Consuls, in the formula, *Videant consules ne quid respublica detrimenti capiat.*

### 2. Lesser Magistrates.

134. **Ædiles.** Two Curule and two Plebeian, forming one board, with the general superintendence of the police, the public buildings, the games, &c. The Curule Ædileship could not be held before the age of 37.

135. **Quæstors.** The number was gradually increased from two to forty; they had the charge of the finances. The Treasury, *Ærarium*, was in the Temple of Saturn.

136. **Tribunes of the People.** Five, then ten in number; entering upon office the fourth day before the Ides of December. The office was established at the first secession of the Plebeians, B. C. 494, to defend them (*Auxilium*) against the arrogance of the Patricians. The Tribunes were inviolable, *sacrosancti*, and practically irresponsible. They had the *Intercessio*, or right of "Veto" upon any action of a

magistrate within the city (except the Dictator), the power to fine or imprison factious opponents, and the right of holding the *Comitia Tributa* (§ 142), *agere cum plebe;* they also acquired the right of sitting in the Senate. Their powers were greatly reduced by Sulla, but afterwards in a measure restored. Their attendants were called **Viators.**

137. **Triumviri Capitales** or **Nocturni.** The police officers of the city. — The attendants of the magistrates were called **Apparitores,** including *Lictors* (§ 130), *Viators* (§ 136), *Heralds, Scribes,* &c.

### 3. The Empire.

138. Under the Empire the magistrates of the Republic continued as mere forms; the chief executive officers, appointed at will by the Emperor, were: — 1. **Præfectus Urbi,** who had the charge of the public order, acquiring in time the whole criminal jurisdiction. 2. **Præfectus Prætorii,** generally two in number, having command of the Prætorian Cohorts (§ 159). The Imperial Treasury was called *Fiscus.*

---

### III. ASSEMBLIES.

139. The **Senate,** at first an advisory body, came to be the ruling power in the state, the Consuls being only its instruments. All matters of finance, of war, of provincial administration, and the initiative in legislative action, belonged to it. The members were chosen by the Censor-

from among those who had held curule offices, but by Sulla's laws the holding of the Quæstorship and any higher office entitled to a seat for life. The normal number was considered 300; but after Sulla it varied with the number of those who had held magistracies. The leading man in the Senate, as determined by the Censors, was called *Princeps Senātus*. A vote passed by the Senate was called *Auctoritas;* when drawn up in legal form, *Senatus-consultum*. It usually met in the *Curia Hostilia*, or in some temple.

140. **Comitia Curiata**, or Assembly of the Curiæ (§ 123). These were early superseded in their political functions by the *Comitia Centuriata* (§ 141), but were kept up until late times for Patrician purposes, such as Adoption, *Arrogatio*. The *Imperium*, or military power, could be conferred only by them, in the *Lex Curiata de Imperio*, for which purpose they were represented by 30 Lictors. — The **Comitia Calata** were also organized by Curiæ, but were entirely passive, being called together by the *pontifices* (§ 143) to witness wills, be present at the inauguration of the *rex* (§ 147) and *flamens* (§ 148), &c.

141. **Comitia Centuriata**, or Assembly of the Centuries (§ 125), held in the Campus Martius, (because, being the army, it could not meet within the city walls,) and presided over by the Consul. Most of the legislation, and the election of the chief magistrates, belonged to this assembly. In the 3d cent. B. C. a reconstruction of the centuries took place, by which, probably, each *class* (§ 125) received equal power, having two centuries (one of *seniores*, one of *juniores*) from each of the 35 tribes (§ 124). The authority of the

Senate was necessary in order to propose a law (*rogare* or *ferre legem*), which, until passed, was called *rogatio;* the people voted with tablets marked U for *uti rogas* (yes) and A for *antīquo* (no).

142. The **Comitia Tributa** were the Assembly of the 35 Tribes (§ 124), each of which had an equal vote. They chose the Lesser Magistrates, later also the Priests, and acquired by degrees a large share of legislative power. A law passed by this assembly was called *Plebiscītum;* after B. C. 286 a *Plebiscītum* had the force of a *Lex*.

## IV. PRIESTHOODS.

### 1. THE GREAT COLLEGES.

\*\*\* These, with the exception of the *Epulōnes*, were at first restricted to the Patricians, but afterwards thrown open to the Plebeians also.

143. The **Pontifices,** eight in number, increased by Sulla to fifteen; at their head the **Pontifex Maximus.** They formed the most important of these bodies, being the acknowledged head of the Roman religion, and having authority over all the other priesthoods. They had power to decide on the legality of any measure or proceeding, and a control over the ritual of the state.

144. The **Epulones,** originally three, increased by Sulla to seven. They had the charge of the sacred feasts, the chief of which was that of Jupiter Capitolīnus (§ 173).

145. The **Decemviri sacris faciundis**, increased by Sulla to fifteen (*Quindecimviri*). They had the care of the Sibylline Books, which they consulted in all public exigencies.

146. The **Augurs**, nine in number, made fifteen by Sulla. They had the interpretation of the *Auspices;* viz. *ex cœlo* (thunder and lightning); *ex avibus* (called *oscĭnes* when they sang, *alĭtes* when they flew); *ex tripudiis* (from the feeding of chickens); *ex quadrupedibus;* and *ex diris* (from prodigies). The auspices (*greater* or *lesser*) belonged to the magistrates (see § 129), but were interpreted by the augurs, who thus acquired great political influence, being able even to break up the Comitia, or declare their action void. — The **Haruspices** were an inferior body, originally Etruscan, who examined the entrails of the beasts sacrificed, and explained prodigies and lightning.

2. The Patrician Colleges.

147. The **Rex Sacrificulus** (cf. King Archon, § 94) had the highest rank in the state, but no political power. He was appointed after the expulsion of the kings, to perform the religious rites which had belonged to them.

148. The **Flamens** were priests devoted to the service of some special deity. They were fifteen in number, at the head of whom stood the *Flamen Dialis* (of Jupiter), *Martialis* (of Mars), and *Quirinalis* (of Quirīnus).

149. The **Salii** were priests of Mars Gradīvus (§ 60), twelve in number, having charge of the *Ancilia* or sacred shields. They made an annual procession (§ 173), leaping, singing, and beating the shields with rods.

150. **Fetiales** (§ 71), twenty in number, the chief being called *Pater Patratus*. They had the care of the public faith, performed the ceremonies at the declaration of war, &c. In later times, Plebeians of high rank seem to have been admitted into the College.

## V. COLONIES, &c.

151. **Roman Colonies** were composed of Roman citizens, who were provided with land (from $1\frac{1}{2}$ to 7 *jugera*, § 189) in a conquered country, without losing their citizenship.

152. **Latin Colonies** were military posts, composed of Latins or of Romans who were willing to lose a portion of their civic rights in consideration of a grant of land. They had a *quasi* independence, but stood in a relation of inferiority. Only four were sent out after the Second Punic War, their place being then taken by Roman Colonies, which had before fallen into disuse.

153. **Municipia.** These were Italian towns which received Roman citizenship (§ 161) in whole or in part. In the last century of the republic the term was applied also to colonies. — The **Præfectura** was a town whose laws were administered by a Præfect sent out by the Roman Prætor. — Villages and smaller towns were called *Fora* (market-towns), *Conciliabŭla*, *Vici*, and *Castella*.

154. **Provinces.** These were conquered countries, ruled as subject, paying tribute, and governed at first by Præ-

tors, afterwards by Proconsuls and Propraetors (§§ 130, 131). Augustus divided them into *Senatorial* and *Imperial*, the latter being those which required military administration (see p. 24).

---

## VI. MILITARY AFFAIRS.

### 1. Before Marius.

155. The **Legion** consisted of 4200 men,—1200 **hastati**, young men; 1200 **principes**, middle-aged men; and 600 **triarii**, or veterans; to whom were added 1200 **velites**, or light-armed: there were, besides, 300 **equites**, or cavalry. The *hastati* formed the front line, the *princĭpes* the second, while the *triarii* were a reserve. The command of the legion was held by six **tribuni militum**, two months by each in turn.

156. The infantry of each legion was divided into 30 **maniples**, ten to each line, each maniple consisting of two **centuries**, among which the *velĭtes* were equally distributed, 20 to each century. Thus, of the *hastati* and *princĭpes* each maniple contained 120 heavy-armed soldiers and 40 *velĭtes*, forming 20 in front and 8 deep (the century having 10 men in front); while the maniple of the *triarii* contained only 60 heavy-armed soldiers and 40 *velĭtes*. Each century was commanded by a **centurion**, the *centurio prior* (of the right-hand century) commanding the whole maniple. The centurion of the first (right-hand) century of the *triarii* was called *primipīlus*.— The *equites* were divided into 10 **turmæ**.

157. The heavy-armed soldiers were clad in the brazen helmet (*cassis*), shield (*scutum*), cuirass (*lorīca* or *thorax*), and greaves (*ocreæ*); they carried the short two-edged Spanish sword (μάχαιρα), and a javelin (*pilum*), in place of which last, the *triarii* carried a spear (*hasta*). The *velītes* wore a leathern helmet (*galea*), and carried a buckler (*parma*), Spanish sword, and several darts (*hastæ velitāres*).

## 2. Reform of Marius.

158. This consisted in substituting the organization by **cohorts** for that by maniples. The division into *hastati*, &c. (§ 155) was given up, and the legion contained only infantry, the cavalry being furnished by the allies as *auxiliaries*. The legion consisted therefore of 10 cohorts of three maniples each. Each maniple had 20 men in front by 10 deep, so that the cohort contained 600 men, the legion 6,000. All the legionary soldiers were in full armor, carrying the Spanish sword and the *pilum*. The silver eagle was now made the standard of the legion.

---

159. The **Prætorian Cohort** was a select body of men acting as body-guard to the commander. Under the Empire the Prætorian Cohorts formed a standing army stationed at Rome, where they had an immense camp. It came in time to be the ruling power in the state.

160. The camp was made in the form of a rectangle, with two streets running at right angles through the middle point, *groma*. At the points where these touched the walls

were the four gates, the **decumana**, turned from the enemy, the **prætoria**, towards the enemy, and the **principalis dextra** and **sinistra**, at the right and left hand; the front part of the camp being where the legionary soldiers were posted, — towards the *decumāna*. The **Prætorium**, or headquarters, was in the same part, in the middle of the chief street.

160½. After a successful campaign in a legitimate war, *justum bellum*, against foreign foes, in which the dominion of the state had been extended, and 5,000 of the enemy slain in a single battle, the *Imperator* received by decree of the Senate the honor of a **Triumph**. He entered the city in a splendid procession, at the head of his army, and proceeded to the temple of Jupiter Capitolīnus to offer sacrifice. — The **Ovation** was an inferior kind of Triumph.

---

## VII. LAW.

161. **Civitas.** Full citizenship, *Jus Quiritium* (§ 122), consisted in, — 1. *Public rights*, i. e. (1.) Jus Suffragii, the right of voting; (2.) Honorum, of holding office; (3.) Provocationis (§ 162); and 2. *Private rights*, i. e. (4.) Connubii, of intermarriage, and (5.) Commercii, of trade. — The civil condition of a man was called his *caput*; *capitis deminutio* was any loss of citizenship in whole or in part. *In tabulas Cærītum referri*, or to become an *Ærarius*, was to lose the right of suffrage; *tribu moveri* seems to signify

to be transferred to a less honorable tribe (§ 124), a punishment often inflicted by the Censors (§ 132).

162. **Provocatio.** The right of appeal to the people from the decision of any magistrate (except in early times the Dictator, § 133), in cases in which the punishment was death, scourging, and afterwards heavy fines. This was looked upon as the bulwark of Roman liberty. Appellatio was the appeal to one magistrate from the decisions of another.

163. **Twelve Tables.** The laws made by the Decemvirs, B. C. 451, after an examination of Grecian institutions. These formed the foundation of Roman law; many ameliorations of the ancient severity were introduced (see §§ 164, 165).

164. **Matrimonium.** The Patrician marriage was by confarreatio, in which a cake made of spelt, *far*, was carried before the bride. The wife came thus into the *manus* or unlimited power of the husband. — By the laws of the Twelve Tables (§ 163), marriage by usus, or cohabitation, was made valid; but by passing once a year a space of three nights (*Trinoctium*) out of her husband's house, the wife avoided the *manus*. — Another method was coemptio, or purchase by *mancipatio* (§ 166).

165. **Patria Potestas.** The son as well as the wife was in the *manus* (§ 164) of the Paterfamilias, which gave power of life and death. By the Twelve Tables (§ 163) he could escape the *manus* by being thrice sold as a slave and emancipated (*manu mittere*); the first two times he returned into his father's *manus*, the third he remained free.

This *Patria Potestas* extended to all sons, with their families, and all unmarried daughters.

166. **Mancipatio.** A formal sale, made in the presence of five or more witnesses. It was employed in the sale of *res mancipî*, i. e. real estate, slaves, cattle, and children; other property being *res nec mancipî*. By this process Quiritarian ownership (*dominium ex jure Quiritium*) was conveyed.

167. **Nexum.** A contract for debt, entered into by formalities similar to those of *mancipatio* (§ 166), by which on non-payment, with interest commonly at ten per cent, the debtor came into the creditor's power, who could make him work for him, keep him in chains, sell him into foreign lands (*trans Tiberim*), or put him to death. An Addictus was one who came into the relation of servitude to his creditor by regular process of law. The *Nexus* and *Addictus* were not slaves, but in a servile condition. — **Mutuum** was a contract for debt resting on the mere transfer of money from one to another.

168. **Agrarian Laws.** The public land obtained by conquest was under the management of the Senate, and usually divided among its members for a low rent. This was called Occupatio; the property of the land still remained in the state, but the occupiers came in time to consider it as their own, and it was bought and sold as such. The object of the various agrarian laws was to give the public land, in patches of generally seven *jugera* (§ 189), to the poorer citizens; this was called Assignatio. Tiberius Gracchus carried such a law, B. C. 133.

169. **Sumptuary Laws.** Laws passed at various times to check the growth of luxury, by prohibiting display and lavish expenditures.

170. **Parricidium,** originally the murder of a parent, came by degrees to signify any murder. — **Proditio,** *treason,* was aid given to a foreign enemy. — **Perduellio,** such hostile actions as endangered the institutions of the state, such as usurpation of kingly authority (Sp. Cassius), interference with the rights of the Tribunate (Ti. Gracchus), &c. Such crimes came under the laws *de Majestate* (i. e. anything touching the sovereignty of the state).

171. Courts. The Prætors (§ 131) conducted trials, as well criminal as civil. *Quæstiones Perpetuæ,* or special criminal courts, were established, the first for Extortion (*Res Repetundæ*), B. C. 149; others for Bribery, Treason, Adultery, Counterfeiting, &c. — The court of the **Centumviri** (three from each tribe, § 134) had jurisdiction in cases of inheritance. — The judges (*judices*) in the *Quæstiones,* ordinary or special, were originally taken from the Senators; by a law of C. Gracchus, B. C. 121, from the Equestrian Order (§ 126); Sulla restored the privilege to the Senators; and a law, B. C. 70, enacted that they should be taken equally from *Senators, Equites, and Tribuni Ærarii* (§ 172). — *Diem dicere* signified to charge a person with any crime, and appoint a day for bringing the matter to trial. The judges voted with tablets marked A for *absolvo,* C for *condemno,* and N L for *non liquet.*

172. Revenue. This was derived chiefly from the provinces, and was managed by the Censors (§ 132). The

public domain, consisting of arable and pasture lands and mines, *metalla*, was let. (The rent of the pasture-lands, *pascua*, was called *scriptūra*.) Besides this, the provinces paid a fixed sum, *stipendium*, to the treasury. But Sicily and Asia, instead of the *stipendium*, paid *vectigalia*, consisting chiefly of the tithes, *decŭma*, on agricultural produce: the collecting of these was let out to *publicani*. — The **Tributum** was an extraordinary property tax (cf. εἰσφορά, § 104) on Roman citizens, paid back when the exigency was passed. It was raised in the Tribes (§ 124), by officers called *Tribuni-Ærarii*. The *Vicesima* was a tax of twenty per cent on inheritances and manumissions. The harbor duties were called *Portorium*.

## VIII. FESTIVALS.

### 173. Feriæ Statīvæ. *Fixed Festivals.*

Mar. 1. — Kal. Mar. — Procession of the **Salii** (§ 149) to Mars Gradīvus (§ 57), continuing several days.

" 17. — 16 Kal. Apr. — **Liberalia**, to Liber (§ 64), *toga virīlis* (§ 184) assumed.

Apr. 21. — 11 Kal. Mai. — **Palilia**, to Pales (§ 74); founding of the city.

May 1. — Kal. Mai. — Festival of Bona Dea (§ 72) by the women.

" 17. — 16 Kal. Jun. or  
" 27. — 6 " } **Ambarvalia**; Procession of the Fratres Arvales to bless the fields.

July 6. — Prid. Non. Jul. — **Ludi Apollinares,** lasting 8 days.
" 15. — Id. Jul. — **Transvectio Equitum,** annual procession of the knights (§ 125) in honor of Castor and Pollux (§ 82).
Aug. 21. — 12 Kal. Sept. — **Consualia,** to Consus (§ 62). Rape of the Sabines.
Sept. 15. — 17 Kal. Oct. — **Ludi Romani or Maximi (Circenses)**; for five days.
Nov. 14. — 18 Kal. Dec. — **Epulum Jovis in Capitolio** (§ 144).
" 15. — 17 Kal. Dec. — **Ludi Plebeii (Circenses),** lasting 3 days.
Dec. 17. — 16 Kal. Jan. — **Saturnalia,** to Saturn (§ 70), lasting 3 days.
Feb. 15. — 15 Kal. Mar. — **Lupercalia,** feast of purification (§ 74).
" 17. — 13 Kal. Mar. — **Quirinalia,** the disappearance of Romulus.
" 23. — 7 Kal. Mar. — **Terminalia,** to Terminus (§ 66); riginally the end of the year; boundaries re-established.
" 24. — (§ 206.) — **Regifugium,** to celebrate the expulsion of the kings.

174. The **Feriæ Latinæ,** an annual ceremony of great solemnity, were *Feriæ Conceptīvæ,* i. e. on a day appointed by the consuls. The **Ludi Sæculares,** in honor of Apollo, were celebrated once in a hundred years.

# MISCELLANEOUS.

*₊* We present a general view of the parts of the ship, house, dress, &c., giving the Greek and Roman names side by side.

### 175. Ship, *Navis*, Ναῦς.

Prow, *prora*, πρώρα.
Beak, *rostrum*, ἔμβολος.
Mast, *malus*, ἱστός.
Yard, *antenna*, κέρας.
Deck, κατάστρωμα.
Anchor, *ancŏra*, ἀγκύρα.

Stern, *puppis*, πρύμνη.
Rudder, *gubernaculum*, πηδάλιον.
Sail, *velum*, ἱστίον.
Oars, *remi*, κῶπαι.
Keel, *carīna*, τρόπις.
Sheets, *pedes*, πόδες.

The *Cheniscus*, χηνίσκος, was an ornament at the prow, the *Aplustre*, ἄφλαστον, at the stern. The larger ropes were called *funes*, σχοινία; the smaller, τοπεῖα.

176. Ships were named from the number of banks of oars, *Monēres, Biremes, Triremes*, &c. The *Trireme* was chiefly used during the height of Grecian power, the *Quinquereme* during the Roman period.

### 177. House, *Domus*, Οἰκία.

The peculiarity of the Greek house was its division into two portions, the **Andronītis** for the men, and the

Gynæconītis for the women; the former was towards the front. The principal feature of both Roman and Grecian houses was the large hall, Atrium or Cavædium, αὐλή, open to the air. In this the Roman received his friends; here were the images of his household gods, *simulacra*, and of his ancestors, *imagines*. The opening in the roof above was called Compluvium: in the *Tuscan Atrium* (the earliest style) this was formed simply by the beams of the house; otherwise it was supported by pillars. The Impluvium was a cistern in the floor, to catch the rain. About the *Atrium* were the various rooms. The Triclinium was the dining-room, in which couches were placed about three sides of a table, and usually three reclined upon each couch.

### Temple, *Templum*, Νεώς.

178. The principal apartment of the Temple was the *Cella*, Ναός; in large temples there was also a vestibule, Πρόναος, and chamber in the rear, ὀπισθόδομος, in which the treasures were kept. Temples, like houses (§ 177), were usually lighted by an opening in the roof, ὕπαιθρον; hence called *hypæthral*. They commonly had columns in front, at both ends, or all around (a *peristyle*), when they were called *peripteral*. The number of columns in front was regularly *even*, from two to ten in number; on the side, the Greek temples had *twice as many columns as in front, and one more;* e. g. the Parthenon (100 feet wide), being *octastyle*, had 17 columns along the side. Roman temples, on the other hand, had *twice as many intercolumniations on the*

*side as in front;* thus, an octastyle temple, having 7 intercolumniations in front, had 14 on the side, and consequently 15 columns. There were also circular temples. Temples usually faced east or west.

179. There were properly three orders of architecture: the **Doric**, distinguished for massiveness and simplicity; the **Ionic**, for grace; the **Corinthian**, for richness of ornamentation. The gable was called the *Pediment*, and the space between the pediment and columns the *Entablature*, which was divided into the *Cornice*, jutting out just below the pediment, the *Frieze*, usually adorned with sculpture, and the *Architrave*, resting immediately on the column. The frieze was in the Doric order divided by perpendicular mouldings, *triglyphs*, into spaces called *metopes*. — The **Tuscan** order was a modification of the Doric; the **Composite**, an inelegant mixture of Ionic and Corinthian, used in Rome during the Empire.

## Theatre.

180. The Theatre was divided into the *Stage*, *Orchestra* (corresponding to our *parquet*), and *Cavea*, κοῖλον. The *Scena*, σκηνή, was the wall back of the stage, on which was the scenery of the play, the curtain rising immediately in front of it. The stage proper was called *Proscenium*, and was always in view of the spectators. The Orchestra was used in Greek theatres for the chorus, and contained the θυμέλη, an altar of Dionȳsus. In Roman theatres it was occupied by Senators and other distinguished persons. The *Cavea* was formed of concentric rows of seats, rising one above another, with parallel passages called *præcinctiones*,

διαζώματα, and divided by transverse stairways into wedge-shaped compartments called *cunei*. In the Grecian theatre the orchestra formed a complete circle, in the Roman, only a semicircle.

181. Amphitheatres were elliptical in shape, the *cavea* being divided in the same general manner as in theatres. The central part was called the *arēna*, and was used for gladiatorial combats; sometimes it was flowed with water for the exhibition of mock sea-fights. It was surrounded by a massive wall of masonry: above this was a balcony, called the *podium*, where the Emperor and other distinguished persons sat. — When the people wished the life of a vanquished gladiator saved, they turned their thumbs down; when one was wounded, they cried out, "*Habet.*"

182. Plough, *Aratrum*, Ἄροτρον.

Yoke, *jugum*, ζυγόν.
Pole, *temo*, ῥυμός.
Share, *vomer*, ὕννις.
Mould-boards, *aures*.
Coulter, *culter*.
Share-beam, *dentāle*, ἔλυμα.
Handle, *stiva*, ἐχέτλη (held with the right hand).
Plough-tail, *buris*, γύης (with the left).

### Dress.

183. The chief article of dress was the *tunic*, χιτών; the *Doric chiton* had no sleeves, and reached about to the knees; the *Ionic* had sleeves, and reached to the feet. The tunic was fastened round the waist with a girdle, *zona*, ζώνη; long tunics and sleeves were thought effeminate.

184. The peculiar Roman dress worn over this was the

*toga* (*gens togata*), a long rounded shawl, thrown over both shoulders, but in such a manner that it could fall down in front, its folds forming the *sinus*, and leave the right arm free. The *toga virīlis*, assumed by young men at the age of 16 (§ 64), was of the natural color of the wool; while that of candidates for office, *toga candida*, was whitened artificially. The *toga prætexta* had a broad purple border, *latus clavus;* it was worn by children and the higher magistrates. Matrons wore the *stola*, reaching to the feet, instead of the toga. The Greeks wore in its place the *pallium*, ἱμάτιον, which was rectangular, or the χλαμύς (scarf), which was oblong, and more delicate than the pallium. — The *paludamentum* was the military cloak worn by officers, the *sagum* being that of the common soldiers and of the northern nations; the *pænŭla* was a travelling-cloak.

185. *Braccæ* (trousers) were only worn by barbarians (*Galli braccati*). — Sandals, *solea*, or *sandalium*, σάνδαλον, and shoes, *calceus*, ὑπόδημα, were worn on the feet; the shoes of Senators were adorned with a small crescent. — On the head was worn a felt cap, *pileus*, πῖλος, or hat, *petăsus*, πέτασος.

# TABLES.

*⁎* In these tables the modern values are given approximately, for loose and ordinary calculation. The decimal system generally prevailed in Greece, the duodecimal in Italy.

## MEASURES OF LENGTH.

186. THE unit of measure was the *Foot*, the Grecian being a little larger, the Roman a little smaller, than the English.

### Grecian.

| | | |
|---|---|---|
| 4 Finger-breadths, Δάκτυλος, | = 1 Palm, Παλαιστή, | = 3+ in. |
| 3 Palms | = 1 Span, Σπιθαμή, | = 9+ in. |
| 4 Palms | = 1 Foot, Πούς, | = 12.135 in. |
| 2 Spans | = 1 Cubit, Πῆχυς, | = 1½+ ft. |
| 2½ Feet | = 1 Step, Βῆμα, | = 2½+ ft. |
| 6 Feet | = 1 Fathom, Ὀργυιά, | = 6+ ft. |
| 10 Feet | = 1 Calămus, Κάλαμος, | = 10+ ft. |
| 100 Feet | = 1 Plethrum, Πλέθρον, | = 100+ ft. |
| 6 Plethra | = 1 Stadium, Στάδιον, | = 1— furlong. |
| 30 Stadia | = 1 Parasang, Παρασάγγης, | = 3½— m. |

*⁎* The *span* was originally the distance from the tip of the thumb to that of the middle finger; the *cubit*, from the elbow to the tip of the middle finger; the ὀργυιά, between the outstretched arms.

### 187. Roman.

The true Roman subdivision of the foot was duodecimal, into 12 inches; but the Grecian measures, the finger-breadth (*digĭtus*) and palm (*palmus*), were also employed.

| | | |
|---|---|---|
| 12 Inches, *Uncia*, | = 1 Foot, *Pes*, | = 11.65 in. |
| 18 Inches | = 1 Cubit, *Cubĭtus*, | = 1½— ft. |
| 2½ Feet | = 1 Step, *Gradus*, | = 2½— ft. |
| 5 Feet | = 1 Pace, *Passus*, | = 5— ft. |
| 10 Feet | = 1 *Decempĕda* | = 10— ft. |
| 120 Feet | = 1 *Actus* | = 120— ft. |
| 1000 Paces | = 1 *Miliarium* (*Mille passuum*) | = 1— mile. |

### MEASURES OF SURFACE.

188. The Grecian unit was the *Plethrum* (the square of the linear *Plethrum*, § 186); the Roman, the *Jugĕrum* (twice the square of the *Actus*, § 187).

#### Grecian.

| | | |
|---|---|---|
| 100 Square Feet | = 1 Ἄκαινα | = 100+ ft. |
| 25 Ἄκαιναι | = 1 Ἄρουρα | = 9⅓+ rods. |
| 4 Ἄρουραι | = 1 Πλέθρον | = 1— rood. |

### 189. Roman.

The *Actus Simplex* was a strip of land 120 feet by 4.

| | | |
|---|---|---|
| 5 Actus | = 1 Uncia | = 8+ rods. |
| 1½ Unciæ | = 1 Clima | = 12+ rods. |
| 4 Climăta | = 1 Actus Quadrātus | = 1+ rood. |
| 2 Actus Quadrati (12 Unciæ) | = 1 Jugĕrum | = 2+ roods. |
| 200 Jugĕra | = 1 Centuria | = 124+ acres. |

## MEASURES OF CAPACITY.

190. The Grecian and Roman measures correspond so nearly that we give them side by side. The *Cyăthus*, Κύαθος (⅓ gill), is common to all.

### Liquid.

| | | | | | |
|---|---|---|---|---|---|
| 6 Cyăthi | = | 1 Hemĭna, Κοτύλη, | = | ½— pt. |
| 2 Hemĭnæ | = | 1 Sextarius, Ξέστης, | = | 1— pt. |
| 6 Sextarii | = | 1 Congius, Χοῦς, | = | 3— qt. |
| 8 Congii | = | 1 Roman Amphŏra | = | 6— gal. |
| 12 Χόες | = | 1 Ἀμφορεύς, or Μετρητής, | = | 9— gal. |

### 191. Dry.

| | | | | | |
|---|---|---|---|---|---|
| 6 Cyăthi | = | 1 Hemĭna, Κοτύλη, | = | ½— pt. |
| 2 Hemĭnæ | = | 1 Sextarius, Ξέστης, | = | 1— pt. |
| 2 Ξέσται | = | 1 Χοῖνιξ (only Greek) | = | 1— qt. |
| 16 Sextarii | = | 1 Modius, Ἑκτεύς, | = | 1— peck. |
| 6 Ἑκτεῖς | = | 1 Μέδιμνος (only Greek) | = | 1½— bu. |

### WEIGHTS.

192. The Roman pound, *Libra*, was about equal to three fourths of the Attic *Mina*. The values are given in terms of the Avoirdupois scale.

### Grecian.

| | | | | | |
|---|---|---|---|---|---|
| 6 Obŏli | = | 1 Drachma | = | 2+ dr. |
| 100 Drachmæ | = | 1 Mina | = | 1— lb. |
| 60 Minæ | = | 1 Talent | = | 57 lb. |

193. This table is that of the Attic silver weights, the *Drachma* = 66.5 Troy grains. This was the system most in use during the flourishing period of Greece. The values can be reduced to either of the other principal systems, according to the following ratios:—

    Attic (Solonian) : Æginétan (Babylonian) : : 3 : 5
    Attic : Eubóic (Old Attic Ante-Solonian) : : 72 : 100
    Æginétan : Eubóic                           : : 6 : 5

## 194. Roman.

The unit was the *As* or *Libra*, divided into twelve ounces, *Unciæ*. The aliquot parts of the As are the *Sextans, Quadrans, Triens, Quincunx, Semis, Septunx, Bes, Dodrans, Dextans,* and *Deunx;* equivalent respectively to 2, 3 &c. *Unciæ*.

    24 Scrupŭla   =   1 Uncia   =   1— oz.
    12 Unciæ      =   1 As or Libra   =   12— oz.

## MONEY.

195. As money was originally reckoned wholly by weight, the denominations of weight (§§ 192–194) were also applied to the money system of the Greeks and Romans, and continued to be so employed even after changes in the standard. The *Drachma* was the unit in the Grecian currency, the *Sestertius* (Sesterce) in the Roman. In comparing Roman with Grecian money, the *Denarius* (= 4 Sestertii) was considered equivalent to the Drachma; it was really equal

to ⅔ Drachma. As, in antiquity, silver was worth nearly a half more in relation to gold than at the present time, the value of the gold coins in the following tables is not reckoned from the silver currency, but given absolutely as compared directly with American gold.

### 196. Grecian.

| | | |
|---|---|---|
| 7 Lepta (Λεπτόν) | = 1 Chalcus, Χαλκοῦς, | = $ 0.004— |
| 8 Chalci | = 1 Obol, Ὀβολός, | = .03+ |
| 6 Obols | = 1 Drachma, Δραχμή | = .18+ |
| 20 Drachmæ | = 1 Stater, Στατῆρ, | = [5.33] (§ 195) |
| 100 Drachmæ | = 1 Mina, Μνᾶ, | = 18.00+ |
| 60 Minæ | = 1 Talent, Τάλαντον, | = 1080.00+ |

197. The Lepton and Chalcus were copper coins; the Obol and Drachma, silver; the Stater (= the Persian *Daric*), gold; the Mina and Talent were not coined, but were denominations of value. Probably no gold was coined in Greece until the time of Alexander, but the Persian daric was extensively used.

### Roman.

198. The money of the Romans was in early times wholly copper, the unit being the *As*. This was nominally a pound, but actually somewhat less, in weight, and was divided into twelve *Unciæ*. In the 3d cent. B. C. the As was reduced by degrees to one twelfth of its original value. At the same time silver coins were introduced; the *Denarius* = 10 Asses, and the *Sestertius*, or *Sesterce* (*semis*

*tertius*, represented by IIS, or HS, = *duo et semis*) = $2\frac{1}{2}$ Asses. The Sestertius, being probably introduced at a time when it was equal in value to the original As, came to be used as the unit (hence *nummus* was used as equivalent to Sestertius); afterwards, by the reductions in the standard, four Asses became equal to a Sesterce. Gold was introduced later, the *Aureus* being equal to one hundred sesterces. — *Sestertium* (M) = 1000 *Sestertii* was used as an expression of value, not as a coin.

199. In the statement of sums of money in cipher, a line above the number indicated thousands; lines at the sides also, hundred-thousands. Thus IIS. DC. = 600 Sestertii. IIS. $\overline{\text{DC}}$. = 600,000 Sestertii, or 600 Sestertia. HS. $|\overline{\text{DC}}|$ = 60,000,000 Sestertii. With the numeral adverb, hundred-thousands are also understood; as *decies, decies IIS.*, or *decies sestertium*, that is, *decies centēna millia sestertiûm*, or ten times a hundred Sestertia = 1,000,000 Sestertii.

200. The following table applies to the last two centuries B. C.:—

| 4 Asses | = | 1 Sestertius | = | $ 0.04+ |
|---|---|---|---|---|
| 4 Sestertii | = | 1 Denarius | = | .16+ |
| 25 Denarii | = | 1 Aureus | = | [5.15] (§ 195) |
| 1000 Sestertii | = | 1 Sestertium | = | 40.00+ |

[Decies Sestertium = $ 40,000.]

# TIME.

## Grecian.

201. The Greeks computed time by Olympiads of four years, following the celebration of the Olympic games (§ 112), which began each Olympiad. The celebration of the games in B. C. 776 was the first one employed for this purpose; in order, therefore, to reduce Greek dates to years before Christ, *the number of whole Olympiads past* (i. e. the date diminished by one) *must be multiplied by four, and* the *product subtracted from* 776. This will give the first year of the given Olympiad. E. g. the third year of the 79th Olympiad : $78 \times 4 = 312$ ; $776 - 312 = 464$. B. C. 464 being the first year, the third will be 462. This is the only method which was universal in Greece; individual states also reckoned by their magistrates, as the Archon in Athens (§ 94), and Ephor (§ 107) in Sparta.

202. The division into months was very various. The Athenian year began at the summer solstice, and was divided into twelve months, half of them *full*, i. e. of 30 days, half *hollow*, of 29 days. Thus in an ἐννεαετηρίς, or cycle of eight years, there would be a loss of ninety days, which were inserted as intercalary months in the 3d, 5th, and 8th years of the cycle.

203. The Attic months were : —

| | | | |
|---|---|---|---|
| 1. Ἑκατομβαιών, | 30 days, | | July; |
| 2. Μεταγειτνιών, | 29 " | | August; |
| 3. Βοηδρομιών, | 30 " | | September; |

| | | | |
|---|---|---|---|
| 4. Πυανεψιών, | 29 days, | | October; |
| 5. Μαιμακτηριών, | 30 " | | November; |
| 6. Ποσειδεών, | 29 " | | December; |
| 7. Γαμηλιών, | 30· " | | January; |
| 8. Ἀνθεστηριών, | 29 " | | February; |
| 9. Ἐλαφηβολιών, | 30 " | | March; |
| 10. Μουνυχιών, | 29 " | | April; |
| 11. Θαργηλιών, | 30 " | | May; · |
| 12. Σκιροφοριών | 29 " | | June. |

The intercalary month was inserted after Ποσειδεών, and called Poseideon second.

204. The month was divided into three decades, which were called respectively ἱσταμένου μηνός, μεσοῦντος μηνός, and φθίνοντος μηνός. The first day of the month was νουμηνία, and the following days were named regularly in order, δευτέρα, τρίτη, &c. ἱσταμένου μηνός. The same designation was adopted in the second decade, the 11th being called πρώτη μεσοῦντος μηνός, or ἐπὶ δέκα. The 20th was called εἰκάς, and the days of the third decade were reckoned either forward from this, or more frequently backward from the last day of the month; as πρώτη, δευτέρα, &c. ἐπὶ εἰκάδι, or ἐννάτη, δεκάτη, &c. φθίνοντος μηνός; the last day itself being named τριακάς, or ἔνη καὶ νέα.

## Roman.

205. Roman Chronology was reckoned from the building of the city, the date of which was assigned by Varro to B. C. 753. In order, therefore, to reduce Roman dates to

those of the Christian era, *the year of the city is to be subtracted from* 754; e. g. A. U. C. 708 = B. C. 46.

206. Until the time of Cæsar, that is, until B. C. 46 inclusive, the Roman year consisted of four months of 31 days (*Mars*, which was the first month of the year, *Maius*, *Quintīlis*, afterwards called *Julius*, and *October*), seven of 29 days, and one (*Februarius*) of 28 days. [The cause of this arrangement was the Roman superstition in favor of odd numbers.] Every other year an intercalary month (*Mercedonius*), of alternately 23 and 22 days, was inserted, the former after the 24th of February (Feast of *Regifugium*, § 173), the latter after the 23d (Feast of *Terminalia*, § 173; the *Regifugium* falling on these years after the intercalated days). The remaining four or five days of February were added to the *mensis intercalāris*, which thus always had 27 days, February being on these years reduced to 24 or 23 days.

207. This complicated and inconvenient system was reformed by Cæsar, who abolished the intercalary month, added ten days to the year (two each to *Januarius*, *Sextīlis* [*Augustus*], and *December*, one each to *Aprīlis*, *Junius*, *September*, and *November*), and once in four years intercalated a day, after the 24th of February (*Regifugium*), or 6th day before the Kalends of March, hence called *bis sextum*. This is the Julian Calendar, which continued in use until amended in modern times by the Gregorian Calendar.

208. The first day of each month was called *Kalendæ*, from *calare*, to call; that being the day on which the priests publicly announced the new moon in the *Comitia Calata*

(§ 140), which they did, originally, after actual observation. Sixteen days before this, that is, on the 15th day of March, May, July, and October, but the 13th of the other months, came the *Idus*, or day of the full moon; eight days before the Ides were the *Nonæ*. The month was thus divided into three weeks of eight days, and one of five or seven. The days were reckoned backward from these points; but as it was the custom of the Romans always to include the point of departure in such calculations, it is necessary, in order to find the day of the month, to take this into account. Thus, the day before the Kalends, Ides, &c., is called *Pridie Kalendas*, &c.; the day before this, *ante diem* (a. d.) *tertium Kalendas*, &c. Therefore, with the Kalends, *two must be added to the number of days of the preceding month; with the Nones and Ides, one must be added to the day of the month on which they occur, and the day of the date must be taken from the number thus obtained.* E. g. the sixth day before the Kalends of November: 31 (the number of days of October) $+ 2 = 33$; $33 - 6 = 27$. The date will be Oct. 27. — The third day before the Ides of March: $15 + 1 = 16$; $16 - 3 = 13$. March 13.

209. The months of the Roman year were originally ten, the sun's course not being taken into account. Afterwards two were added, January (month of *opening*) and February (of *purification*), to bring the lunar year into agreement with the solar.

210. The days of the year were divided into, — 1. **Dies Fasti,** 38 in number, when the Prætor might hold his court. 2. **Dies Comitiales,** 184 in number, when the Comitia might

be held. 3. **Dies Nefasti,** when neither courts nor Comitia could be held; these were, for the most part, devoted to some religious service, being thus Dies Festi. 4. **Dies Festi,** dedicated to the gods. 5. **Dies Profesti,** appropriated to the business of men. 6. **Dies Intercisi,** 65 in number, on which certain hours were *fastus*, others *nefastus*. The same term is applied to days which were partially *festi*.

---

### 211. WINDS.

| | | | | | |
|---|---|---|---|---|---|
| N. | Septentrio, | Ἀπαρκτίας. | S. | Auster, | Νότος. |
| N.E. | Aquilo, | Βορέας. | S.W. | Africus, | Λίψ. |
| N.E. | Vulturnus, | Καικίας. | W. | Favonius, | Ζέφυρος. |
| E. | Subsolānus, | Ἀπηλιώτης. | N.W. | Caurus, | Ἰάπυξ. |
| S.E. | Eurus, | Εὖρος. | N.W. | Circius, | Θρακίας. |

### 212. ROMAN PRÆNOMENS,
#### WITH THEIR ABBREVIATIONS.

| | | | |
|---|---|---|---|
| A. | Aulus. | Mam. | Mamercus. |
| App. | Appius. | N. | Numerius. |
| C. | Caius. | P. | Publius. |
| Cn. | Cneius. | Q. | Quintus. |
| D. | Decimus. | Ser. | Servius. |
| K. | Cæso. | Sex. | Sextus. |
| L. | Lucius. | Sp. | Spurius. |
| M. | Marcus. | T. | Titus. |
| M'. | Manius. | Ti. | Tiberius. |

# GENEALOGIES.

## MYTHOLOGICAL.

### 213.

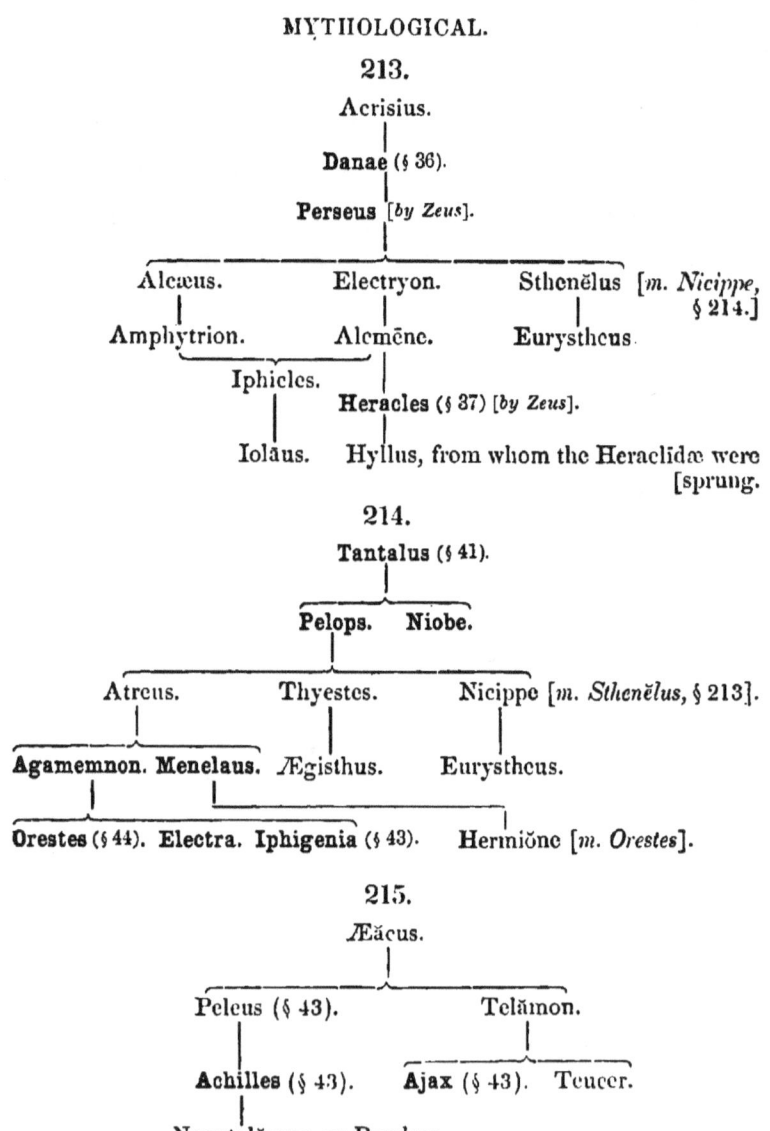

Acrisius.
|
Danae (§ 36).
|
Perseus [by Zeus].
|
―――――――――――――――――――――――――
Alcæus.           Electryon.        Sthenělus [m. Nicippe,
   |                 |                           § 214.]
Amphytrion.        Alcmēne.         Eurystheus
   ⎵―――――――――――――⎵
   Iphicles.       |
         |      Heracles (§ 37) [by Zeus].
      Iolāus.   Hyllus, from whom the Heraclidæ were
                                         [sprung.

### 214.

Tantalus (§ 41).
|
―――――――――
Pelops.   Niobe.
   |
――――――――――――――――――――――――――
Atreus.        Thyestes.       Nicippe [m. Sthenělus, § 213].
   |              |                 |
―――――――――      Ægisthus.        Eurystheus.
Agamemnon. Menelaus.
   |           |
Orestes (§ 44). Electra. Iphigenia (§ 43).   Hermiŏne [m. Orestes].

### 215.

Æăcus.
|
――――――――――――――
Peleus (§ 43).       Telămon.
   |                    |
Achilles (§ 43).   ―――――――――
   |               Ajax (§ 43).  Teucer.
Neoptolĕmus, or Pyrrhus.

## GENEALOGIES.

### 216.

Deucalion (§ 34) [m. Pyrrha].
├── Hellen.      Amphictyon.
│   ├── Dorus.  Xuthus.  Aeolus.
│   │           └── Achæus.  Ion.

### 217.

Dardănus.
│
Erichthonius.
│
Tros.
├── Ilus.           Assarăcus.        Ganymede (§ 12).
│   │               │
│   Laomĕdon.       Capys.
│   │               │
│   Priam (§ 42).   Anchises.
│   │               │
│   Hector, etc.    Aeneas (§ 43).

### 218. KINGS OF PERSIA.

Cyrus the Great, B. C. 559 – 529.
├── Cambyses, B. C. 529.   Atossa, m. Darius I. (Hystaspes), B. C. 521.
│                          │
│                          Xerxes I., B. C. 485.
│                          │
│                          Artaxerxes I. (Longimănus), B. C. 465.
│                          │
│   Xerxes II., B.C. 425.  Sogdianus, B.C. 425.  Darius II. (Nothus), B.C. [423.
│                                                │
│   Artaxerxes II. (Mnemon), B. C. 404.  Cyrus the Younger.  Ostanes.
│   │                                                        │
│   Artaxerxes III. (Ochus), B. C. 362.                      Arsames.
│   │
│   Arses, B. C. 339.  Darius III. (Codomannus), B .C. 336.

# GRECIAN.

## 219. ALCMÆONIDÆ.

Megacles, the opponent of Pisistrătus.
|
Clisthenes (§ 92).        Hippocrătes.
|
Megacles.    Agariste [m. Xanthippus, who command-
|                                       ed at Mycăle, B. C. 479].
Dinomăche, m. Clinias, killed B.C. 447.   Pericles (§ 92).

Alcibiades, the general, d. B. C. 404.

## 220.

Cypsĕlus  =  the same wife  =  Stesagŏras.
|                                |
Miltiădes (tyrant of the Chersonese).    Cimon.

Stesagŏras II.   Miltiades (Marathon, B. C. 490).
|
Çimon (R. Eurymedon, B. C. 466).

## 221. SPARTAN KINGS.

Their common progenitor was ARISTODEMUS, of Heraclid descent, whose two sons, EURYSTHENES and PROCLES, were the ancestors of the Agid and Eurypontid lines (§ 106).

| AGIDÆ. | EURYPONTIDÆ. |

ANAXANDRIDES, B. C. 560.           ARISTON, B. C 560.

CLEOMENES, LEONIDAS, B.C. 491. Cleombrŏtus,   DEMARATUS,
B. C. 520.         (Thermopylæ.)    Regent for Pleistarchus.   B. C. 510.

PLEISTARCHUS,  Pausanias, Regent.    LEOTYCHIDES, B.C. 491.
B. C. 480.        (Platæa, B. C. 479.)  (descended from another branch
                                          of the line).

Cleomĕnes, guard. of  PLEISTOANAX, B.C. 458.   Zeuxidāmus.
his nephew Pausanias.

PAUSANIAS, B. C. 408.               ARCHIDAMUS, B. C. 469.

AGESIPOLIS, CLEOMBROTUS, B. C. 380.  AGIS,  AGESILAUS, B C 394.
B. C. 394.     (Killed at Leuctra, B.C. 371.)  B. C. 429.   (Coronea, B. C. 394.)

AGESIPOLIS,   CLEOMENES,       ARCHIDAMUS,
B. C. 371.    B. C. 370.        B C. 361.

## 222. FAMILIES OF ANTIGONUS AND ANTIOCHUS.

**Antigonus**, general of Alexander, *d.* B. C. 310.
- Demetrius I. (Poliorcētes) of Macedon, *m.* sister of Cassander, [*d.* B. C. 283.]
  - Demetrius of Cyrēne.
  - **Antigonus Gonatas.**
    - **Antigonus Doson**, k. of [Maced., *d.* B. C. 221.]
    - Stratonice I.
    - Phila., da. of Sel. I.
      - Demetrius II.
        - Philip V. of Macedon.
          - Perseus, k. of Maced., conquered by Æm. Paulus, [B. C. 168.]
      - Stratonice II.

Antiochus, gen. of Philip II.
- Seleucus I. Nicātor, *d.* B. C. 281.
  - Antiochus I. Soter, son of Sel. I. [and Apama.]
    - Antiochus II. Theos (children of Antiochus I. (and Strat. I.)
      - Seleucus II. Callinicus.
        - Antiochus III. the Great, *d.* B. C. 187.
          - Seleucus IV. Philopātor, *d.* B. C. 175.
            - Seleucus IV. Philopātor, *d.* B. C. 175.
              - Demetrius I. Soter, k. of Syria.
              - Laodice.
          - Antiochus IV. Epiphanes, [*d.* B. C. 161.]
            - Antiochus V. Eupātor.
        - Seleucus III.

# GENEALOGIES.

223.

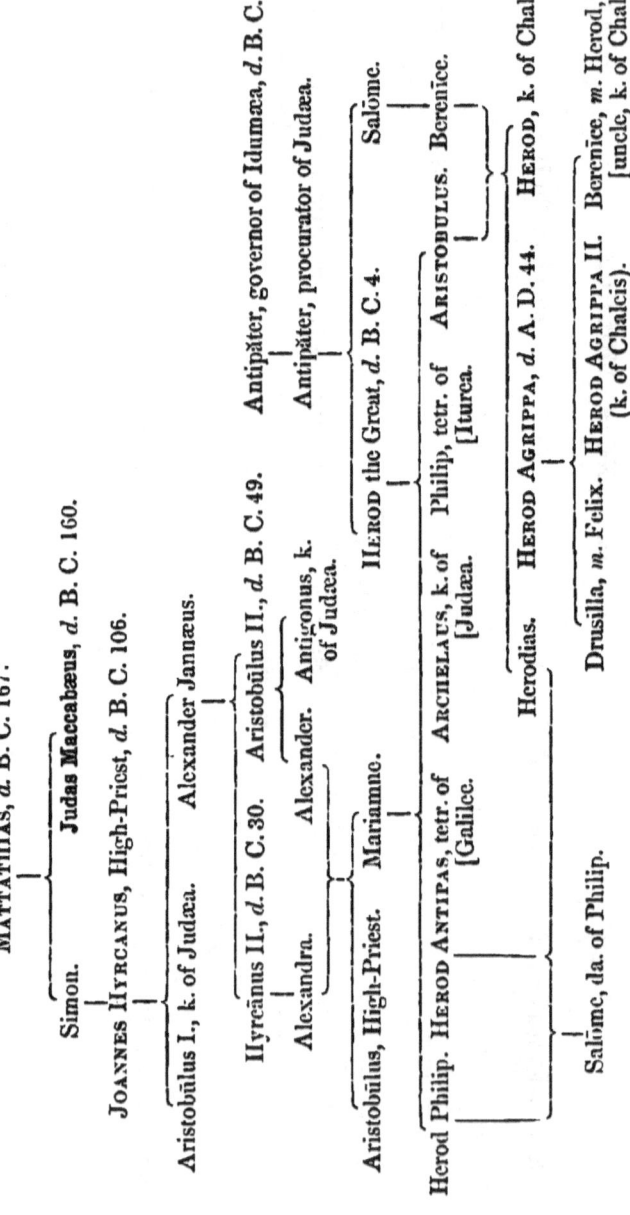

# ROMAN.

## 224.

```
L. Cornelius Scipio Barbatus, cos. B.C. 298.
 │
 L. Cornelius Scipio, cos. B.C. 259.
  ├── Cn. Scipio Calvus, cos. B.C. 222.
  │     └── P. Scipio, cos. B.C. 218.
  │           ├── P. Corn. Scipio Africanus Major.
  │           │     └── (by Æmilia, dau. of L. Æmilius Paulus, fell at Cannæ;
  │           │          sister of L. Aemilius Paulus Macedonicus)
  │           │           ├── P. Scipio Africanus.
  │           │           │     └── Younger son, adopted by .. P. Scipio Africanus
  │           │           │          under the name of
  │           │           │          **P. Scipio Aemilianus Africanus Minor.**
  │           │           └── Cornelia, m. Ti. Sempronius Gracchus.
  │           │                 ├── Sempronia.
  │           │                 ├── Ti. Gracchus.
  │           │                 └── C. Gracchus.
  │           └── L. Corn. Scipio Asiaticus.
  └── 1. **P. Scipio Nasica** (§ 80), cos. 191.
         └── 2. P. Scipio Nasica Corculum, cos.
               [B.C. 162, 155; pont. max.
               └── 3. P. Scipio Nasica Serapio, cos. B.C.
                     [138: pont. max.: mur-
                     derer of Ti. Gracchus.
                     └── 4. P. Scipio Nasica, cos. 111.
                           ├── 5. P. Scipio Nasica, prætt. 94.
                           │     ├── Licinia.
                           │     │     └── L. Licinius Crassus Scipio,
                           │     │          adopted by Crassus, the orator.
                           │     └── (sister) — L. Licinius Crassus, the orator.
                           │           └── Licinia, m. C. Marius.
                           └── Q. Caecilius Metellus Pius Scipio,
                                adopted by Q. Metellus Pius.
```

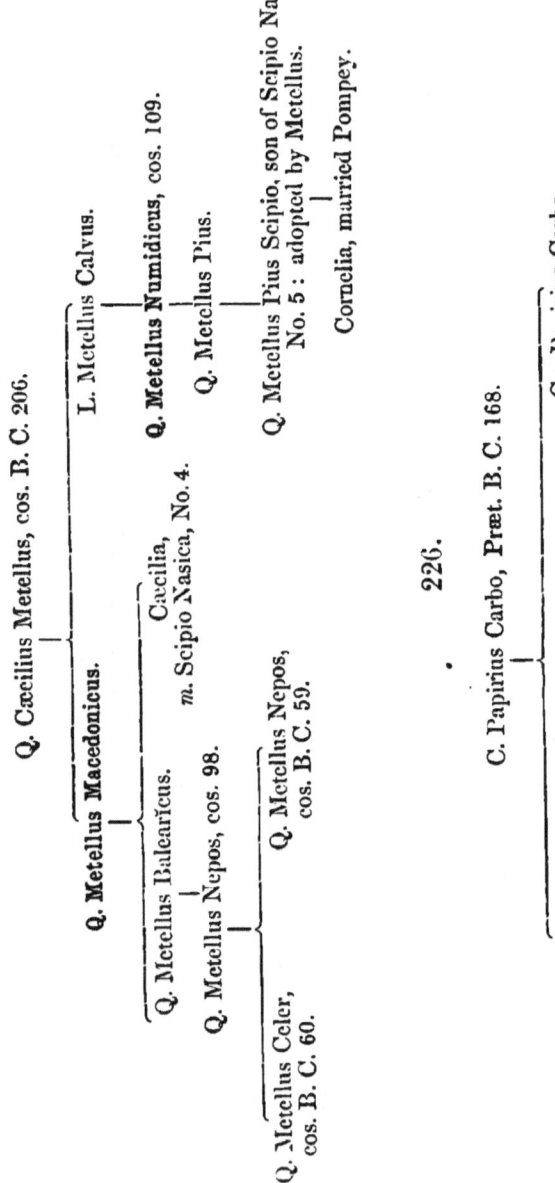

# GENEALOGIES.

## 227.

Q. Mucius Scævola, Præt. B.C. 215.
- Q. Mucius Scævola, cos. B.C. 175.
  - P. Mucius Scævola, cos. B.C. 175.
    - P. Licinius Crassus Dives Mucianus, Pont. Max.: cos. B.C. 131, adopt. by P. Licin. Crassus Dives.
  - P. Mucius Scævola, Pont. Max.: cos. B.C. 133.
  - **Q. Mucius Scævola, Pont. Max., cos. B.C. 95.**
- Q. Mucius Scævola, cos. B.C. 174.
  - **Q. Mucius Scævola,** (Augur,) cos. B.C. 117.

## 228.

Augustus, married
1. Scribonia.  2. Livia.

From Scribonia:
- Julia, married **M. Vipsanius Agrippa**.
  - **Agrippina 1.** — Germanicus
    - Agrippina 2. — Cn. Domitius Ahenobarbus
      - **Nero.**
    - **Caligula.**

Octavia, sister of Augustus, m.
1. C. Marcellus.  2. **Mark Antony**.
- M. Marcellus.
- Antonia 1. married L. Domitius Ahenobarbus.
  - Cn. Domitius Ahenobarbus (see above)
- Antonia 2. married Drusus.
- Domitia Lepida, married M. Valerius Messala.
  - Valeria Messalina.

From Livia:
Tiberius Claudius Nero, married to Livia.
- **Tiberius**, m. Julia, da. of Augustus.
- Drusus, married to Antonia 2.
  - Germanicus.
  - **Claudius** married Valeria Messalina.
    - Octavia. Britannicus.

www.ingramcontent.com/pod-product-compliance
Lightning Source LLC
Chambersburg PA
CBHW020107170426
43199CB00009B/428